What works for young people leaving care?

What works for young people leaving care?

Mike Stein

Published by Barnardo's
Tanners Lane
Barkingside
Ilford
Essex
IG6 1QG

Charity registration no 216250

© Barnardo's, 1997; Mike Stein, 2004

First published 1997
Second edition 2004

Designed and produced by Andrew Haig & Associates

Printed in the United Kingdom by Russell Press, Nottingham

A catalogue record for this book is available from the British Library

ISBN 1 904659 08 X

Contents

About the author

Mike Stein is Professor of Social Work and co-Director of the Social Work Research and Development Unit at the University of York. For the past 25 years he has been researching the problems and challenges faced by young people leaving care and, recently, the experiences of young people living on the streets and running away from care. He was involved in the preparation of the Guidance on Leaving Care for the Children Act 1989 and the Children (Leaving Care) Act 2000, as well as training materials to accompany both Acts. Since 1997 he has, at different times, been an advisor to Who Cares?, the National Association of Young People in Care, A National Voice and First Key. He has published extensively in the field and been consulted by government, local authorities and voluntary organisations on the development of leaving care services in England, Scotland and Northern Ireland as well as internationally.

Acknowledgements

It has been my good fortune to work with a first-class team for many years. Nina Biehal, Jim Wade and Jasmine Clayden go back 15 years, and not far behind – nearly 10 years – Ian Sinclair, my co-Director of SWRDU at York, and, more recently, Jo Dixon. They have all contributed significantly to the development of knowledge about young people leaving care. Also from our Unit, Dawn Rowley has assisted greatly with the preparation of the manuscript. Many others have contributed, too many to mention all of them individually. Di McNeish was the Barnardo's driving force behind both editions. Caroline Davies and Chris Sealey from the Department of Health provided the opportunity for research funding and the bridge between research, policy and practice. John Pinkerton, from Queen's University, Belfast, has offered wise external counsel for many years. Finally, I am indebted, as ever, to all those young people, whose lives have not been easy, but who have been prepared self-lessly to share them with researchers, and thus who made this publication possible.

1 Introduction

What works for young people leaving care? The simple answer, from a scientific perspective, is nothing, or more precisely, we don't know, in terms of what has been proven using the methodological gold standard of randomised controlled trials. I can hear the outcry from practitioners before the proverbial ink is dry: randomised controlled trials? Yet another ethically impoverished researcher with no respect for our professional judgement and beliefs, allocating our clients by chance to receive or be denied a service. Totally unacceptable. And I can hear another outcry from some of my sociology colleagues: typical atheoretical do-gooder, unreconstructed positivist, simply no point in engaging him in the epistemological arguments underpinning the interpretative position. Well I can't say I'm too sorry about that. But surely not another outcry? What about a more pragmatic approach to research? Why not study leaving care work as it is practised, rather than setting up and investigating special experiments? Now that dose of reality suddenly sounds very attractive. Or is it just a cop out? I will return to these issues later but let me ask the opening question to a different constituency.

What works for young people leaving care? The simple answer, from a practitioner perspective, is everything, or more precisely a belief by leaving care workers in what they are doing and in their effectiveness. There are certainly many different types of schemes to assist care leavers. However, I have to confess to a slight unease if the names of the projects reflect different philosophies and diverse methods of working. For example, we have 'Never Alone' and 'On Your Own' projects. We have 'Stepping Out' and 'Stepping In' projects. And internationally, well let's be straight, in the USA – where else? – they have 'Attachment' as well as 'Emancipation' schemes. Can they all work? Let us for the time being be benevolent about belief. They could all work, or at least bits of them could work, couldn't they?

It was belief which motivated many of the early philanthropists, including Dr Barnardo, to rescue homeless and orphaned pauper children from the streets and workhouses of London during the second half of the nineteenth century. Barnardo initiated the setting up of village homes for young women, as well as fostering schemes and lodging houses for older children and young people. He also pioneered some of the earliest leaving care schemes, placing girls 'in service' and boys in the 'services' or as industrial apprentices. But it was also belief that led to what was in effect the compulsory emigration of rescued children to the Empire, as a testing ground for the new 'environmental' philosophy to which Barnardo was committed – as well as meeting the population and labour needs of the new colonies.

> If the children of the slums can be removed from their surroundings early enough, and can be kept sufficiently long under training, heredity counts for little, environment counts for everything. (Barnardo, in Heywood, 1978, p53)

Indeed, emigration was seen by most of the rescue societies of the day as an opportunity for the 'children of the slums' to make a fresh start. But, as we now know, it did not always work out like that for the children despatched to Australia, Canada and South Africa:

> I hated it. I cried myself to sleep every night. I was cut off from all the friends I ever had. Here's me, a slip of a kid, cooking for seven shearers … I worked like a navvy. And they had seven children I had to wash and clean for … I got one weekend off in six and the rest of the time I was working. (Pamela, in Bean and Melville, 1989, p23)

These were the words of Pamela, a 15-year-old girl 'placed' in an outback Australian farming household, whose fate not only included domestic slavery, but being the victim of attempted rape by the eldest son. Perhaps not surprisingly, she became obsessed about her lack of family:

> I got to the stage where I thought there's just no hope; I'm never going to find anyone. But, you know, surely there must be somebody, somewhere I'm related to … I was getting desperate feeling you're nobody, you're nothing. (Pamela, in Bean and Melville, 1989, p25)

In 1924 an official committee concluded that many of these children, like Pamela, had become cheap labour, were poorly prepared and had little contact with the organising charities after immigration. But despite the committee's condemnation, the practice continued until as recently as the early 1960s.

Recent research has also revealed how many of these children were deceived about their parents' existence. And although some had built successful careers – and there is historical evidence of upward mobility in comparison to those who remained at home – they often faced psychological problems which originated from their separation and lack of knowledge about their past, particularly about their parents and their brothers and sisters (Parr, 1980; Bean and Melville, 1989). All of which raises important methodological questions: whose outcomes are we concerned with – society's, the agencies', or the young person's?

Belief and commitment have been the moving force behind many progressive developments in the field of childcare in recent years. But at the same time they have led to philosophies and related practices in children's homes that have left some children, young people and adults psychologically damaged for life. The use of regression therapy in Leicestershire's children's homes and the so-called 'pindown' system of control in operation in selected Staffordshire homes were, in effect, sanctioned abuse. As forms of 'treatment' they were not hidden or secret practices, but existed openly within their departments, and were advocated with evangelical zeal by their principal architects (Stein, 1993). Listening to the haunting revelations of young adults abused in children's homes during the last three decades has all but reduced 'leaving care' to a euphemism.

> I was beaten up until I started crying, then I was put on a social worker's knee and I would have to tell them the root of my problems. (Young man remembering regression therapy, in his evidence to the Leicestershire Inquiry, Dorman, 1992, p8)

> Susan was put into 'pindown' when she was 9 years old. 'Susan admitted – very basic programme, be very nasty to her' (logbook entry). Susan was required to wear pyjamas and kept in a sparsely furnished room. She was not allowed contact with other children and was not permitted to attend school. She was required to knock on the door before going to the toilet. (Levy and Kahan, 1991, p109)

For these victims perhaps we should speak of 'surviving care' although, sadly, not all have done so. The tragic irony of their situation is obvious: many of these children were rescued from abusive or neglectful parents to be provided with 'care' (Utting, 1991; 1997; House of Commons, 2000; Colton, 2002).

To return to the ethical objections to research raised by practitioners in the opening paragraph. If we need an ethics to regulate research interventions, do we not also need an ethics to regulate interventions without research? And what should the relationship be between belief and research? Charles Booth, in his pioneering studies of poverty in London at the turn of the century, captured this perceptively when he wrote:

> In intensity of feeling and not in statistics lie the power to move the world. But by statistics must this power be guided if it would move the world right. (Charles Booth, 1889, cited in Fraser 1976, p127)

But how, from a research perspective, are we to establish what works? This seemingly simple question opens up one of the most complex and sustained methodological debates – qualitative versus quantitative research – and their underlying paradigms. As Shaw has argued, the inter-relationship of qualitative and quantitative methods transcends methodological choices: 'it raises questions about causes and meaning; single cases or comparison; context as against distance; homogeneity and heterogeneity; validity and the criteria of quality in social work research; the relationship of researcher and researched; and measurement' (Shaw and Gould, 2001, p29). Perhaps it is unsurprising then that there are heated debates among the advocates of these different approaches, although increasingly there is recognition of the need for different types of research designs in evaluating social work interventions (Sinclair, 2000).

There is also recognition that 'research knowledge' – although a broad church of perspectives and paradigms – is only one source of knowledge that may influence and shape social care. Pawson and colleagues (2003) propose a five source based classification: organisational knowledge; practitioner knowledge; user knowledge; research knowledge and policy community knowledge.

This exploration of what works for young people leaving care will, in the main, be informed by 'research knowledge', although the boundaries between the different knowledge sources are not always distinct, especially in descriptive accounts of policy and practice. The main research designs introduced in this text will be:

Studies with quasi-experimental designs
The main foci of these designs will include: research into the outcomes of leaving care schemes using a participation group of scheme users and a 'naturally' occurring matched comparison group of young people being looked after but not being assisted by schemes; research comparing the outcomes of different leaving care services and independent living programmes; and research following up young people living in, and leaving, foster care placements using different instruments to test outcomes (research studies will include Biehal et al, 1995; Cook, 1994; Dixon and Stein, 2002; Pecora et al, 2004; Pinkerton and McCrae, 1999; Sinclair et al, 2003). Although

these studies may not be able to provide the same reliability of evidence as randomised controlled trials (RCTs), particularly in respect of controls for selection and external sources of bias, they can, through rigorous design, contribute to attributive confidence – an evidence-based understanding of different practice interventions.

Studies with non-experimental designs

Several such studies will be drawn upon in this text. Indeed, as has been suggested already in the 'What works?' series, perhaps the bulk of social welfare research falls into this category (Beresford et al, 1996). Non-experimental designs are evaluated interventions – for example, of leaving care projects – with no random allocation and no pre-intervention matching of groups, and, indeed, most often without a comparison group at all. The results of single project evaluations are at best suggestive. However, as Macdonald and Roberts have pointed out:

> Attributive confidence can be enhanced in two ways. Firstly, if a number of such studies featuring a range of clients in different circumstances produce similar results, then one can feel confident that the intervention is influencing the changes. Secondly, if experimental studies featuring similar procedures and approaches already exist, we can have more confidence in interpreting the results of pre-experimental studies. (Macdonald and Roberts, 1995, p13)

User studies, ethnography and personal accounts

The view from below, as the substantive focus of research, or as part of other research studies, features prominently in this publication. Knowing how those collectively, and often patronisingly, referred to as 'cases' view, experience and feel about being on 'the receiving end' is essential to providing good quality services – particularly as guides to the kinds of activities and the kinds of qualities people want (Timms, 1973; Mayer and Timms, 1970; Fisher, 1983; Who Cares? Trust, 1993). To have evidence-based social work without the evidence from a user perspective seems unthinkable. Yet there are not inconsiderable methodological problems – for example, of gaining critical perspectives, of selected perceptions of sub-strata, and, perhaps more pertinently, of correlating the user views of service providers with pre-intervention goals:

> She was really nice that lady, we had some good chats, but now you ask me I am not really sure why she used to come and see me ... perhaps she was a bit lonely ... but I did like her. (Stein, 1997, p10)

These problems point to the need for greater methodological sophistication and variety in understanding the social worlds of those receiving services. For without this grounded understanding it would be difficult to conceptualise acceptable interventions, and thus plan quantitative studies including RCTs. In this context there have been some recent attempts to develop ethnographic work and life course theory to explore young people's in-depth experiences of leaving care – biographical stories in specific social contexts and between multiple lines of action (Baldwin, 1998; Horrocks, 2002). A particular focus of these approaches has been described as revealing the way in which 'invisibilities' may have social and developmental consequences for care leavers – that is, trying to capture what care leavers may see as important to them, and why, instead of privileging government outcome data, the 'official knowledge' representation of care leavers' lives (Horrocks, 2002).

Such methodological variety should also include personal accounts of those who have experienced life in and after care (Hitchman, 1966; Arden, 1977; Doyle, 1989; MacVeigh, 1982; Fever, 1994). For although less systematic in their descriptions of interventions, they, as a 'user knowledge' source, may provide the insights and reflections to guide further inquiry. However, this is not to suggest the development of effective services can be determined solely by user studies. They need to be combined with other kinds of evidence.

Surveys
Several surveys are referred to in the text (for example, Biehal et al, 1992; Fry, 1992; Broad, 1998; 2003). As a research method the survey does not enable us to evaluate effectiveness in practice but it does contribute to effective service provision – by providing information about the prevalence in society of particular characteristics, or patterns among selected groups, such as young people leaving care. Surveys can thus provide essential contextual data, for example, on the educational attainment of 16-year-olds in the general population, against which the performance of 16-year-old care leavers can be compared. It can also provide data on specific groups of young people, an essential basis for service planning. Surveys may also be an important source of information from a range of respondents on the implementation of law and policy such as the Children Act 1989 and the Children (Leaving Care) Act 2000.

Cohort studies
Cohort studies, by collecting data from the same people over a period of years, can explore factors in early childhood that seem to be associated with later well-being.

They can help us understand why some children, given a poor start in life, do well. Identifying those factors which seem to have made a difference to the children who have overcome a poor start in life is the first step in ensuring that these protective factors are more widely available. (Macdonald and Roberts, 1995, p18)

Analysis of data from the National Child Development Study (NCDS) – based on an original cohort of 17,773 children born in the first week of March 1958 and subsequently followed up at 7, 11, 16, 23 and 33 years – is presented:

First, to compare the educational and occupational attainments of those who had experienced care with those who had never been in care (Cheung and Heath, 1994). Second, to examine the mental health of adults who had been in care (Cheung and Buchanan, 1997).

The challenge for data analysis is in identifying exactly what is making the difference, or what are the mechanisms for bringing about change, again highlighting the need for both quantitative and qualitative approaches.

Chapter outline

Returning to our initial question, 'what works for young people leaving care?', the different types of studies, outlined above, will be organised around key themes.

Chapter 2 will provide a **context** for the research. This will include an exploration of the background to, and main developments in, leaving care policy between the Children Act 1948 and the Children (Leaving) Care Act 2000, in order to historically locate and assess the contribution of research during this period.

What are the **problems and challenges** faced by young people leaving care? In answering this question, Chapter 3 will first of all present the findings from the mainly small-scale qualitative research studies carried out before 1990 whose foci were primarily upon the problems faced by care leavers in isolation from other young people. It will then discuss studies completed since 1990 that have compared the experiences of care leavers with those of other young people, using comparison samples and secondary data sources.

What **services** are being provided to meet the needs – the problems and challenges – of young people leaving care? Drawing in the main upon descriptive and process studies, Chapter 4 documents the development of specialist leaving care schemes and discusses the different ways of classifying leaving care services.

What are the **outcomes** of leaving care services? There are those who would argue that this is the same question as asking what works for young people leaving care, and that only the use of randomised controlled trials (RCTs) will provide the answer. Others have criticised RCTs on ethical and practical grounds as well as seemingly insurmountable challenges of complexity and cost. However, as Sinclair has argued, we should resist the temptation to dismiss all thought of RCTs and attempt to overcome the difficulties through attention to description, methodological triangulation and replication – which means, as well as RCTs, using other research designs (Sinclair, 2000). Perhaps, because of some of the difficulties and objections outlined above, to date there have been no RCTs of leaving care interventions. However, there have been other kinds of outcome research, particularly those using quasi-experimental designs or established tests, and it is the findings from these studies that are presented in Chapter 5.

What can we learn from research and evaluation about **leaving care practice**? It is this question that will be explored in Chapter 6 by drawing upon the studies introduced in the earlier chapters as well as the evaluation of other project and practice initiatives.

What is the relationship between the body of empirical research introduced so far and **theory**? Not an easy question to answer given the often crude polarisation between empirical research and theory – as well as theory and practice? – and the failure to make explicit the theoretical foundations of empirical work. In exploring this question, Chapter 7 discusses the contribution of attachment theory, focal theory, life course analysis and resilience theory.

In conclusion, Chapter 8 revisits the initial question: what works for young people leaving care? In response, the main arguments and evidence are summarised as well as pointers for further research.

Key messages

- Belief and commitment have led to many progressive child welfare developments but they have also contributed to the abuse of children and young people in care.
- Interventions should be based upon research knowledge of what works.
- This should include studies with different research designs.

2 Research in context

Young people leaving care are first and foremost young people, and as such their destiny is in part shaped by the opportunities, policies and attitudes that are common to all young people. Indeed, their high degree of vulnerability to unemployment and homelessness during the 1980s was an indicator of major structural and social policy changes affecting young people more generally in society. More recently, the large number of unaccompanied asylum-seeking and refugee young people who are looked after or supported by local authorities is a reminder that child welfare is no longer a parochial affair immune from the impact of global events. These wider contextual influences and constraints have interacted with a more parochial child welfare agenda, and the agency and actions of many, including young people themselves, in the making of leaving care policy. This chapter tells the story of the main developments in leaving care policy in England and Wales from the Children Act 1948 to the Children (Leaving Care) Act 2000, in order to provide a context for the research findings discussed in subsequent chapters (Stein, 1999).

Aftercare and Children's Departments 1948–1971

The Children Act 1948, based upon the recommendations of the Curtis Committee, created the new Children's Departments. A single Committee and Department was, for the first time, to have the responsibility for the continuous care of all children deprived of a normal home life. The reforming spirit of 1945 and Labour's social democratic politics provided the ideological climate for the acceptance of welfare policies which reflected a more humane and liberal approach. The harsh morality theory of the Charity Organisation Society with its practice of classifying the 'deserving' from the 'undeserving' and religious and biological determinism had all condemned the poor. In keeping with the new thinking, Section 12 of the 1948 Act finally broke with the poor law status of 'less eligibility' for children in care under which so many children had suffered. The poor law mentality, which shaped much residential childcare during the 1930s, was captured by a Home Office Inspector's report:

> In residential homes, both statutory and voluntary, staff were found to be treating the children as 'lower orders' who did not deserve the ordinary standards of civilised living. In

one home the windows lacked curtains for fear that the children would wipe their noses on them; they were not provided with handkerchiefs. In an Anglican convent home menstruation was not to be mentioned and the girls were given nothing to cope with it so they tore strips from their sheets and face towels. Children had no clothes of their own; often they were assembled in height order and marched to a counter where they received the next day's garments. (Barnardo's, 1987, p9)

The 1948 Act gave local authorities a new duty to 'further best interests ... and afford opportunities for proper development of character and abilities' and 'make such use of facilities and services available for children in the care of their own parents' (Section 12(1) and (2)). This included a new legal framework in regard to the aftercare of young people – a duty to advise and befriend; a power to accommodate; and powers in respect of providing financial assistance towards the costs of accommodation, maintenance, education and training.

In contrast to a rich history on many areas of the work of Children's Departments (see, for example, Heywood, 1978; Packman, 1981) very little is known about aftercare policy and practice, including the fate of care leavers, during this period. We do know that the economic context, particularly from the 1950s to the mid-1970s, was very favourable. After World War II, and following a period of post-war austerity, the economy moved into its boom years – modernity's heyday – providing job opportunities for all young people, all be it within a market reflecting and reproducing existing class and gender divisions.

There was full youth employment during most of these years. Analysis of data from the National Child Development Study (see Chapter 3) revealed that as late as 1976 most young people left school at the minimum school-leaving age of 16 and nine out of ten had secured employment within six months of leaving (Kiernan, 1992). There were jobs on offer for those living in care and leaving school at 15, and, on the raising of the school-leaving age in 1972, at 16. And, indeed, the homes provided for in Section 13 of the 1948 Act became widely known as 'working boys' and working girls' hostels'. Also, between 1948 and 1962, on leaving care at 18, young men were required to do up to two years of National Service, and even until the implementation of the Children and Young Persons Act 1969, in 1971, there were specialist approved schools which trained young men for the services.

Also, a new approach to practice, the childcare officer's social casework, developed during this period. Social casework, derived from psychoanalytic theory, offered the potential for a new non-coercive response (Donzelot, 1980). The work of the child psychiatrists Anna Freud, Donald Winnicott and John Bowlby was very influential. Bowlby's 'maternal deprivation' theory, published in *Child care and the growth of love* became the key work in the training of childcare officers (Packman, 1981). The message of his research was unequivocal: a child needs a warm, intimate and continuous relationship with their mother or mother substitute. Attachment as a concept and a developing theory was to be central to the new casework (see Chapter 7).

Consistent with these findings, and their legal embodiment within the 1948 Act, the philosophy and practice was on rescuing children from institutional care by boarding them out with foster carers or by returning them to the family home. But meeting the needs of deprived children and young people more generally was a foundation stone of the childcare officer's new and developing social casework. And this casework included practice with children and young people in and after leaving care (Frost and Stein, 1989).

Those young people unable to return home normally remained in care until they were 18 years of age and were ready to leave. Indeed, the age of 18 became accepted as the normal age of leaving care in Children's Departments, being derived from legal authority – the expiry age of parental rights resolutions and fit person orders. In this respect, both the law and childcare practice mirrored the accepted age and process of 'rite de passage' for most working-class young people at that time. For 18 was the age when apprenticeships ended and adult wages began, when you could be conscripted, and when you could marry without parental consent.

In working boys' and girls' hostels, help was given in preparing young people through attention to practical and social skills, in finding accommodation and work, and in supporting them after they left care. In some local authorities, childcare officers were appointed solely to work with adolescents, including those leaving care. And, nationally, designated childcare and probation and 'aftercare' officers worked specifically with young people returning from approved schools (Stein, 1999).

The only change to the law in relation to leaving care during this period was as a result of the Children and Young Persons Act 1963. Section 58 of this Act gave local authorities new powers in respect of young people who were in care at 17 years of age – previously it had been 18 – and for those who have left care, and a new power for young people leaving care to be visited as well as to be advised and befriended.

In 1968, the Seebohm Report, in supporting the recommendations of the 1968 White Paper, *Children in trouble*, envisaged that a comprehensive aftercare service could be provided by the new social service departments, but this would require the transfer of, 'many probation and aftercare officers ... to the social services department' (House of Commons 1968, par: 265). An important point – for by 1968 half of the children and young people on licence from approved schools were supervised by the probation and aftercare service (House of Commons, 1968, par: 257).

Social services and leaving care 1971–1989

By the beginning of the 1970s it seemed social work had developed a strong professional identity and a clear vision of the future. The growing influence and power of social work was exemplified by the key role of childcare experts in shaping the Children and Young Persons Act 1969, and, by its contribution to the Seebohm Report, in determining the future organisation of social services. But at the same time as the internal dynamic for professional unity and growth was reaching its peak the external context was changing. The consensus surrounding the belief in the good society was evaporating (Pearson, 1975).

The rediscovery of poverty, greater recognition of a range of social problems including inner-city deprivation, homelessness, ethnic conflict and educational under-achievement combined with challenges to traditional forms of authority and authority relations by 'new' pressure groups and social movements, to point to a far more uncertain future. A professional culture which had stabilised itself around a psychodynamic world view and which focused exclusively upon the pathology of the individual, or family, as both a cause and solution, was being challenged. The new curriculum included anti-psychiatry, deviance theory and Marxism, the new practice welfare rights, community work and advocacy. The total equalled radical social work (Pearson, 1975).

More specifically, the reorganisation of the personal social services and the introduction of the Children and Young Persons Act 1969, both in 1971, far from leading to a comprehensive aftercare service within the new departments, resulted in the decline of specialist aftercare work in many local authorities. The end of the probation service's involvement in aftercare, with no commensurate transfer of resources to the new social service departments as envisaged by Seebohm, the replacement of approved school orders with the new all-purpose care orders, and the related redesignation of approved schools as 'community homes with education', all contributed to the demise of the specialist aftercare officer (Stein, 1999).

Also, specialist work with adolescents, either living in children's homes (now designated Community Homes) or after they left care became a very low priority among the new front-line generic social workers – and many fieldwork practitioners were new and untrained following the Seebohm bureaucratisation of social services. Care leavers became a forgotten group. But it was not too long before their voices were heard. Against the wider background of the major social changes outlined above, as well as the emergence of an embryonic children's rights movement, there was a re-awakening of leaving care in the professional and political consciousness.

From as early as 1973 small groups of young people living in care came together to talk about their experiences of living in children's homes, of being on 'the receiving end'. Local 'in care' groups, the *Who Cares?* project, Black and In Care, and the National Association of Young People in Care in different ways began to unlock the feelings and views of young people about care and in particular the connections between their lives in care and their lives after care (Stein, 1983; Collins and Stein, 1989).

A major theme that emerged from the voices of young people was their lack of power over their lives, for example, in relation to their use of money, their attendance at their own reviews, their opportunities to shop, cook and generally to participate while in care. And the dependency created by care was related to their fears about leaving care.

Young people who participated in *Who Cares?* spoke of, 'constant years of tight held hand and dominant guidance … ', '…of being a child until you are 18 … ', '…of social services planning your life for you…' and 'of being kicked out of care.' And for the first time, through the publication in September 1997 of *Who Cares? Young people in care speak out*, the words of these young people received widespread publicity in the national media, including the popular press and 'The World at One' (Page and Clark, 1977).

A major gap in our knowledge in the post-war period was the absence of any research into aftercare. But this was beginning to change from the second half of the 1970s with the publication of mainly small-scale descriptive studies (Godek, 1976; Mulvey, 1977; Kahan, 1979; Triseliotis, 1980; Burgess, 1981; Stein and Ellis, 1983; Stein and

Maynard, 1985; Lupton, 1985; Morgan-Klein, 1985; Stein and Carey, 1986; Milham et al, 1986; First Key, 1987). The main impact of these studies, discussed in Chapter 3, was to highlight for the first time the problems and challenges experienced by young people leaving care.

Such findings included the lowering of the age at which young people left care, often as young as 16, and were expected to live independently. Changes in childcare law and practice introduced during the 1970s (as a result of the Children and Young Persons Act 1969), contributed to this. For whereas the old approved school orders, parental rights resolutions and fit person orders combined legal prescription and high-level committee authority with normative expectations in determining the age of discharge from care, discretionary welfare, embodied in the new care order, was far more subject to individual social work judgement and external constraint – the latter including pragmatic concerns, such as the pressure on residential care places. An ironic situation given the hopes riding on the new welfare thinking to contribute to a more needs-led practice.

The low priority afforded to these young people in the new generic social service departments has already been commented upon. There was to be little improvement in aftercare services during the 1970s and early 1980s, for against a background of successive child abuse inquiries, child protection work increasingly became the main preoccupation (Parton, 1985). In addition, whereas an emerging welfare model had gone hand-in-hand with the commitment of the pre-Seebohm childcare officer to assist these young people, radical social work and the new curriculum, including the developing children's rights discourse, was a far more contradictory force. It did, as has been argued, provide a climate for the re-awakening of leaving care in the political and professional consciousness, particularly through its support for advocacy and in-care groups. But it was a crude practice nourished on a very basic diet of Marxism (Pearson, 1975). It didn't want to know about residential care, about more bricks in the wall. And even less about those behind the wall.

Also, subsequent policy developments during this period, however progressive in themselves, did not serve these young people well. The persistence of the institutional critique and the closely linked and enduring popularity of community care, both underpinned by a rare academic and political consensus, the rise of the permanency movement to greatly increase the use of adoption and fostering, and the managerial and professional drive to prevent and divert young people from entering care, all reinforced the same message: residential care is bad. And it was – and a lot worse than was realised at the time given recent revelations of physical and sexual abuse (Utting, 1991; 1997; House of Commons, 2000; Colton, 2002).

During these years, residential care increasingly operated in a climate of denial and welfare planning blight, as well as in a philosophical and theoretical void. Young people leaving foster care were not seen as leaving care in a formal sense – the assumption being that they would continue to be supported by their foster carers. In this context, little thought was given to preparation for leaving care or to the type and extent of aftercare support needed. Social service departments were thus, in the main, unprepared for the major changes in society and in social legislation that were to have such a significant impact upon the lives of care leavers.

From the late 1970s onwards there have been profound economic and social changes, changes described and analysed as post-Fordism and, more recently, by the other 'post' – post-modernism (Clarke, 1996). And, whereas the former captures the processes of economic reorganisation in advanced industrial societies, the latter suggests a new post – or late? – modern era of fundamental and complex transformations in the social, economic, cultural and technological spheres (Giddens, 1991). The decline in traditional industries, the development in new technologies and the dramatic rise in youth unemployment during the 1980s had a major impact upon the lives of many young people (Coles, 1995). And, whereas in the past a highly stratified job market had been able to provide opportunities for all, whatever their level of education, the low levels of educational attainment of most care leavers now left them ill-prepared to compete in an increasingly competitive youth labour market. As a consequence a high proportion were unemployed and dependent on some form of benefit and therefore living in, or on, the margins of poverty (Stein, 1997).

In March 1980 the plight of homeless adolescents first became a headline story following the media take-up of Christian Wolmar's article 'Out of care' that appeared in Shelter's magazine *Roof.* The author's combative expose of homeless ex-care young people in London, drifting from hostels to squats to railway arches, led directly to Shelter setting up Homebase (which later became First Key) in response to the, 'inadequate housing provision being made by local authorities for young people leaving care' (Wolmar, 1980). Following Wolmar's revelations, two studies published in 1981 showed that over a third of single homeless people had experienced local authority care (Department of Education, 1981; Scottish Council for Single Homeless, 1981).

The actions and self-organisation of young people themselves, the findings from researchers, the increased awareness by practitioners and managers of the problems faced by care leavers, and the campaigning activities of Shelter and First Key, provided the momentum for a change to the law in relation to leaving care, in which Sections 27–29, 69 and 72 of the consolidating Child Care Act 1980 had remained much the same as the 1948 Act.

The House of Commons Social Services Committee on Children in Care sitting in 1983 provided an opportunity for evidence, which was duly taken up by several organisations including the National Association of Young People in Care. In its 1984 Report (known as the Short Report) the Committee noted:

> The main cause for concern is the considerable variation in the sort of assistance which can be expected, which is at present unacceptably dependent on geographical happenstance. This wide variation in turn arises from the weak and confused state of the law in this respect ... present legislation on continuing care for young people leaving local authority care is diffuse and misleading, and is by nature discretionary rather than obligatory. (House of Commons, 1984: pars 302, 303)

The Short Report recommended strengthening the law in three main areas: by introducing a new duty to prepare young people for leaving care, by a stronger and wider duty in respect of aftercare support, and by prioritising housing need. But perhaps an opportunity was also lost – to recommend new duties in respect of financial assistance. However, radical change was not on the agenda.

After all the evidence had been considered, and the law reviewed, there was only to be one significant obligatory change between the new Children Act 1989 and the old Children Act 1948, a new duty, under Section 24(1), 'to advise, assist and befriend young people who are looked after with a view to promote their welfare when they cease to be looked after'. New permissive powers were introduced under Section 24, 'to advise and befriend other young people under 21 who were cared for away from home' – thus widening the target group for aftercare support, and under Section 27, 'the power to request the help of other local authorities including any local housing authority to enable them to comply with their duties to provide accommodation'. But other than that there was far more of the old than the new in the 1989 Act – the old duty to advise and befriend young people under 21 who were looked after remains, as do the permissive powers to provide financial assistance.

In fairness, it could be argued that the 1989 Act introduced a far more progressive legal framework as a general context for care leavers, given the connections between the lives of young people in families, in care and after care. In this sense, the new provisions for family support services, for the inclusion of children with disabilities, for the recognition of culture, language, racial origin and religion, for consultative rights, for the accommodation of children in need, and for new rights to complain, are all to be welcomed, as is the detailed *Guidance on after-care* (Department of Health, 1991b). But this should not detract from the way that social work policy and practice failed many of these young people during much of this period.

The Children Act and continuing care? 1989–1997

The Children Act 1989, described as, 'the most comprehensive and far reaching reform of child care law which has come before Parliament in living memory', was introduced in October 1991 (Smith, 1989). But, as detailed above, it could not have been implemented at a more difficult time for care leavers – the virtual end of the traditional job market, shrinking housing options, major cuts in welfare benefits and reduced expenditure on public services.

The reform of social security (by the Social Security Acts 1986 and 1988) based on the 'guarantee' of youth training and the assumption that families should take greater financial responsibilities for their young people, ended income support for 16-and 17-year-olds, except in severe hardship, and abolished 'householder status' for under 25s by the introduction of lower rates of income support for this age group. Although campaigning activity by care leavers resulted in exceptions for them to receive income support at 16 and 17 for limited periods, the differential age rates of income support remained in place, resulting in demands on social services to provide 'top-up' payments in order to prevent young people from experiencing extreme poverty, deprivation and homelessness (Action on Aftercare Consortium and Barnardo's, 1996; Stein, 1990).

From the mid-1980s, in response to the increasingly desperate situation facing many young people leaving care, some voluntary organisations and local authorities – but by no means all – pioneered specialist leaving care schemes and projects (Stone, 1990). Planning for the 1989 Act also increased the profile and awareness of leaving care within many authorities, and the introduction of specialist schemes was seen by social services as a way of meeting their new legal responsibilities under the Children Act 1989 (see Chapter 4).

For some local authorities, the Act provided the legislative framework for a comprehensive range of leaving care services, through the provision of specialist leaving care schemes, integrated within an overall general childcare strategy linking care and aftercare. However, the more general picture in England and Wales was of great variation in the resourcing, range and quality of service provision, as well as the complex, inconsistent and discouraging wider social policy framework – confirmed by a wide range of sources including research findings, the Social Services Inspectorate, and the Action on Aftercare Consortium (Garnett, 1992; Biehal et al, 1995; Action on Aftercare Consortium and Barnardo's, 1996; Department of Health, 1997; Broad, 1998).

The Children (Leaving Care) Act 2000

The Labour government, elected in 1997, in its response to the Children's Safeguards Review, following the revelations of widespread abuse in children's homes, committed itself to legislate for new and stronger duties for care leavers. William Utting, who chaired the review, had drawn attention to the plight of 16-year-old care leavers, 'unsupported financially and emotionally, without hope of succour in distress' (Utting 1997).

The proposed changes, detailed in the consultation document, *Me, survive, out there?* were to build upon Labour's modernisation programme for children's services (Department of Health, 1999). This included Quality Protects, National Priorities Guidance, the inspection of leaving care services, good practice guidance, as well as recommending to local authorities research findings to assist them in the development of specialist leaving care schemes.

The Quality Protects initiative, introduced in 1998, provided central government funding linked to specific service objectives. In relation to young people leaving care, objective 5 was to 'ensure that young people leaving care, as they enter adulthood, are not isolated and participate socially and economically as citizens' (Department of Health, 1998).

Three performance indicators linked to this objective were, 'for young people looked after at the age of 16, to maximise the number engaged in education, training or employment at 19; to maximise the number of young people leaving care after their sixteenth birthday who are still in touch … on their nineteenth birthday; to maximise the number of young people leaving care on or after their sixteenth birthday who have suitable accommodation at the age of 19' (Department of Health, 1998).

Also, wider government initiatives to combat social exclusion, including the introduction of the Connexions Service and initiatives to tackle youth homelessness, truancy, under-achievement in education, employment and training, and teenage parenthood are also intended to impact upon care leavers (Social Exclusion Unit, 1998a; 1998b; 1999). Indeed, the changing economic climate combined with the restructuring of post-16-year-old education and training has resulted in reductions in youth unemployment – although there continue to be regional variations, as well as stratification by class, gender, disability and ethnicity, and the continued expansion of low-paid jobs in the service industries: more opportunities and more risks? (Walker, 2002)

Against this background, the Children (Leaving Care) Act was introduced in October 2001. Its main aims are to delay young people's transitions from care until they are prepared and ready to leave; strengthen the assessment, preparation and planning for leaving care; provide better personal support for young people after care; and to improve the financial arrangements for care leavers.

To meet these aims the main provisions of the Act apply to different groups of 'eligible', 'relevant', 'former relevant', and 'qualifying' young people – (see Chapter 2 of the Guidance for a clear explanation of who gets what (Department of Health, 2001a)). The key responsibilities are: to assess and meet the needs of young people in and leaving care; pathway planning; the appointment of a personal adviser to provide advice and support to young people, to participate in needs assessment and pathway planning, to co-ordinate services, to be informed about progress and well-being and to keep records of contact; assistance with education and training up to the age of 24; financial support and maintenance in suitable accommodation; and to keep in touch by the 'responsible authority', that is by the local authority that 'looked after' the young person.

What impact has the Act had in its first two years? Surveys of the work of leaving care teams carried out before and after the Act capture some early changes as reported by leaving care project workers (Broad, 1994; 1998; 2003; Allard, 2002; Hai and Williams, 2004).

First, there has been an increase in the proportion of young people leaving care entering post-16 further education, from 17.5 per cent in 1998 to 31 per cent in 2003. This includes a very small percentage, estimated at around 1 per cent, who entered higher education. Second, and directly linked to the point above, there is a lower proportion of young people not in education, employment or training. In both the 1994 and 1998 surveys this represented around 50 per cent and by 2003 had dropped to 29 per cent (Broad, 1994, 1998).

Third, as regards accommodation, there has been a reduction in the percentage of young people with local authority and housing association tenancies, from 37 per cent in 1998 to 28 per cent in 2003. During the same period there have been increases in the percentages of young people living in supported accommodation and shared or transitional accommodation, from 25 per cent in 1998 to 33 per cent in 2003 (Broad, 1998, 2003).

Fourth, and consistent with Broad's 1998 survey, the planning, availability and provision of health services within leaving care services remained a very low priority. There were only a small number of health staff working in leaving care projects (2 per cent) and very few teams had introduced joint social care and health strategies.

Broad's 2003 survey also explored how leaving care project workers viewed their service before and after the Act. Nearly all of the leaving care teams (over three quarters) that identified their accommodation services as 'average' 'good' or 'excellent' before the Act reported that accommodation had either 'significantly improved' or there had been 'a little improvement' since the Act. But of those (just under a quarter) who saw their service as 'below average' or 'inadequate' before the Act, only two had made any significant progress.

The Act has also been seen by staff as having a positive impact upon the assessment, planning and delivery of financial support as a consequence of the financial transfer to social services and the impact of the Quality Protects initiative. The control and provision of financial incentives has been seen by project staff as contributing to the increase in young people entering further education. However, the survey also found that most 'eligible' and 'relevant' young people were receiving the same level of financial support as young people seeking work and large variations in the amount of leaving care grants and additional weekly allowances being paid to young people. A third of leaving care teams were not providing financial incentives for young people to stay on or move on to further education, training or employment.

Broad's 2002–2003 survey points to a number of more general changes, as seen by project staff.

In each of the areas identified above, where improvement in levels of service was identified, 'assessment functions' were seen as more developed than 'service provision'. Also, the gaps between the higher rated leaving care teams and the lower performers are likely to remain, in part reflecting the historical difference in baseline funding.

The survey also found that services for specific groups of care leavers – young parents, young unaccompanied asylum and refugee seekers, and young people remanded to accommodation – who often have specific needs, were predominantly reported as 'remaining the same' since the introduction of the Act. So that where services were already inadequate they were likely to remain so. However, 'some improvement' was identified for young people with a disability and those post-custody (Broad, 2003).

Research by Allard carried out in two authorities during the first six months of implementation of the Act highlights the strengthening of responsibilities and clarification of roles towards care leavers, and the setting up of dedicated, or specialist, systems, as leading to improvements, especially in the areas of financial support and housing. By contrast, care leavers received lower priority where staff had more general childcare responsibilities, including child protection, where ring-fenced money was being used for other purposes, and where the absences of a dedicated leaving care team resulted in a lack of inter-agency work. The research also highlighted that a lack of placements for under-16s resulted in young people leaving care early and young people clearly recognising the link between their care experiences, good or bad, and what happened to them after care (Allard, 2002).

Research carried out by Hai and Williams in eight London boroughs during the first two years of implementation identified a number of positive developments during that period. There had been an increase in the numbers of social workers and specialist staff working in leaving care teams; needs assessments and pathway plans were welcomed by young people, social workers and their managers; and staff from a range of agencies were more likely to be working with care leavers than before the Act. Leaving care teams also reported greater access to a wider range of suitable accommodation and stronger working relationships with housing providers than before the Act. More problematically, young disabled people were generally denied access to specialist leaving care teams and most boroughs recognised they had difficulties in supporting young asylum-seeking care leavers – often due to their uncertain immigration status, lack of clarity in the divisions of responsibilities between the National Asylum Support Service (NASS) and leaving care teams, and the hostile climate surrounding these young people (Hai and Williams, 2004).

The Act has also been criticised for not including young disabled people in 'respite care' within its provisions. Priestley and colleagues (2003) comment, 'High level respite users may spend so little time at home that it is unrealistic for their parents to take responsibility for preparing and supporting them through the transition to adulthood, even where they are regarded as primary carers' (p867). In their research (see Chapter 3) they also highlight the lack of clarity surrounding young disabled people in 52-week educational or health placements, who although eligible for discretionary aftercare support under the Children Act, rarely receive it through poor communication between services.

These studies provide us with a view from key stakeholders, staff and young people of what has happened since the introduction of the Children (Leaving Care) Act. In doing so they have described the contemporary context. What was beyond the scope of their research designs was an exploration of the relationship between young people's lives before and in care, the post-Act services they received and their outcomes – although such research is in progress and early findings will be discussed in subsequent chapters (Jackson et al, 2003; Dixon et al, 2004).

Key messages

- Research is not carried out in a vacuum. It takes place against a dynamic background of legal and policy developments as well as a wider social and economic context. This chapter has explored the making of leaving care policy between the Children Act 1948 and Children (Leaving Care) Act 2000.
- The post-war egalitarian climate, finally signalling the end of the poor law care of children, provided the context for the Children Act 1948 as well as the childcare officer's social casework. New aftercare duties and powers were

introduced and this led to the development of leaving care services.

- The reorganisation of the personal social services and changes in childcare law, introduced in 1971, led to a decline of aftercare provision and a reduction in the age young people left care, often to as young as 16.

- From the mid-1970s the findings from researchers were to highlight for the first time the problems faced by young people leaving care, and these findings, combined with sustained campaigning, including the actions and self-organisation of young people themselves and increased awareness by practitioners, provided a momentum for change to the law.

- The Children Act 1989 was introduced in October 1991, which, although very progressive in many respects, was far weaker in relation to leaving care. Other than a new duty to prepare young people, the Act, in the main, only extended permissive powers.

- The 1989 Act was also implemented at the most difficult time for care leavers, with the decline of the traditional job market for young people, shrinking housing options, major cuts in welfare benefits and reduced expenditure on public services. However, the Act did raise the profile of the vulnerability of care leavers and led directly to the introduction of more specialist leaving care schemes.

- Research carried out during the 1990s highlighted the weakness of the discretionary powers contained within the Act, as well as the complex, inconsistent and discouraging wider social policy framework, particularly in relation to benefits and housing.

- It was against this background, as well as the revelations of widespread abuse in children's homes, that the incoming Labour government, elected in 1997, committed itself to legislate for new and stronger duties for care leavers as part of its modernisation programme for children's services. In addition, wider government initiatives to tackle social exclusion were also planned to help care leavers.

- The Children (Leaving Care) Act 2000 was introduced in October 2001. Evaluations carried out during the first two years point to an increased take-up of further education; reductions in those not in education, employment and training; a strengthening of leaving care responsibilities and improved funding for leaving care teams. However, divisions between better and poorer funded services have remained. Also there is evidence that young people with disabilities, including those in health and educational placements, were being denied access to mainstream leaving care services, as well as concerns that those

3 **Problems and challenges**

This chapter will explore what research studies tell us about the problems and challenges faced by young people leaving care. This is sometimes referred to as a 'needs assessment' – and may be derived from surveys of representative samples of care leavers and comparison samples of other young people, so that similarities and differences may be identified. However, as well as painting the larger picture, we also need to capture the lives of young people themselves. Qualitative research will help us to begin to explore the 'why' questions raised by these surveys, for example, why do care leavers gain so few qualifications compared to young people who are not looked after? It will also help us to gain a better understanding of the experiences of different groups of care leavers through in-depth interviews.

The chapter will begin with an exploration of the findings from early research studies. It will then discuss the findings of more recent studies, from the 1990s onwards, including those that have made comparisons between care leavers and other young people in relation to leaving care, leaving home and homelessness, education and their post-16 careers. These studies have also contributed to a greater understanding of the experiences of specific groups of care leavers including: young parents; black and minority ethnic care leavers; refugee and asylum-seeking young people; young disabled care leavers; young people with mental and physical health problems; young care leavers who use drugs; and young offenders.

Finally, the chapter will summarise the findings from a review of the literature on the outcomes of former foster young people in the United States.

Early research studies

As detailed in Chapter 2, from the mid-1970s, against a wider background of major social change, as well as the neglect of leaving care within the new social services departments, a body of small-scale qualitative studies increased our awareness of the range of problems faced by young people leaving care and made connections between their difficulties and their pre-care and in-care experiences.

These studies highlighted the diversity of the care experience. They showed that care leavers were not a homogeneous group in terms of their pre-care experiences, their age of entry into care, their care histories, their needs and abilities, or their cultural and ethnic backgrounds. Young people's 'in-care' experiences may have been valued by them and helped them, but they may have also contributed to other problems. They were likely to have experienced further movement and disruption during their time in care, many young people changing placements several times.

For those in longer-term care, there was often a weakening of links with family, friends and neighbourhood. Incomplete information, separation from, or rejection by, those who cared for them, meant that some of these young people were confused about their identity: they often lacked a story of their lives, connecting past and present, which would help them plan for in the future:

> It was bad not knowing my past ... I didn't know my parents' names, I knew their surname but not their Christian names or anything like that. I didn't know my parents at all. That's one thing, that I didn't have a past that I could remember. (Young woman, in Stein and Carey, 1986)

These feelings could be amplified for black and minority ethnic young people brought up in a predominantly 'white' care system, particularly if they became detached from their families and local communities. In 1984, the black poet Lemm Sissay wrote of his care experience:

> I a white boy covered in soot,
> I a black boy kept from me root.
> I born black for a night,
> I born black and forced to be white. (Sissay, 1984)

These early studies also documented young people's poor educational performance, their feelings of being stigmatised by care and their variable preparation for leaving care. And upon leaving care, at between 16 and 18 years of age, loneliness, isolation, unemployment, poverty, movement, homelessness and 'drift' were likely to feature significantly in many of their lives:

> It gets lonely, it's only when you leave care, you know you've been dumped and it's right lonely. (Young woman, six months out of care, living alone, in Stein and Carey, 1986)

As suggested earlier, this picture of needs was derived from small-scale qualitative research, in the main based on selected samples (Godek, 1976; Mulvey, 1977; Kahan,

1979; Triseliotis, 1980; Burgess, 1981; Such et al, 1981; Stein and Ellis, 1983; Stein and Maynard, 1985; Lupton, 1985; Morgan-Klein, 1985; Stein and Carey, 1986; First Key, 1987; Randall, 1988; Randall, 1989; Barnardo's, 1989; Bonnerjea, 1990). Nor were any of the early British studies able to make comparisons with young people from the general population in any systematic way.

The early literature also included a few autobiographical accounts, which provided powerful insights into the lives of their authors growing up in care (Hitchman, 1966; Arden, 1977; MacVeigh, 1982). Janet Hitchman in 1966 reflected on her moves in care as an orphan:

> If reasons and explanations had been given I might have understood, but I doubt it. No one thought of giving explanations to small orphans, any more than to market-bound pigs. (Hitchman, 1966, p12)

The early research studies from the United States, Canada, and other parts of Europe were also limited in size and scope, and at best their findings were impressionistic (McCord et al, 1960; Van Der Waals, 1960; Meier, 1965; Bohman and Sigvardsson, 1980; Raychuba, 1987).

There was, however, one exception, Trudy Festinger's seminal study *No one ever asked us: a postscript to foster care* (1983). Festinger followed up 349 young people who had been discharged from foster and residential group care in New York City in 1975. They had been in care for at least five years – although most had experienced placement disruption and instability – and were aged between 22 and 25 when they were followed up. Many of the experiences and views of the young people were similar to the findings from the early British qualitative research – sometimes uncannily so:

> I wouldn't know my mother if she walked right by me. (Young care leaver, in Festinger, 1983)

> I wasn't aware of being a foster child until aged seven … I learned then because my name was different … but at one time I thought this was true for everyone, that the last name didn't mean anything. (Young care leaver, in Festinger, 1983)

However, in contrast to previous studies, comparisons were made with same-age adults in the population at large. This was achieved by using data from identical questions in two youth surveys, augmented by New York City census data.

There were two main differences between the care leavers and the comparison sample. First, those who had been in care completed less education and gained poorer qualifications. Second, care leavers were less likely to marry or live with a partner. In other respects – perceptions of self and others, health, friendships, dependence on welfare, records of arrest, areas of living – the care leavers, as a whole group, were more alike than different to the comparison sample of 'non-care' young adults. However, there were significant differences between young people leaving foster care and those leaving residential group care. The former, who constituted 75 per cent of the sample, corresponded with the 'more alike' findings outlined above, whereas those leaving residential care (25 per cent) were the most disadvantaged group in respect of education, employment, single parenthood, dependency on welfare and their personal satisfaction rating.

In contrast to Festinger's research, these earlier UK studies left unanswered the question of how the needs of care leavers differed from those of other young people, although gave some signposts for further research.

Research studies: 1990 onwards

More recent research has been able to build upon these earlier studies. Several studies have attempted to compare the experiences of care leavers with those of other young people by the use of comparison samples and secondary data sources. This has included: analysis of the National Child Development Study (NCDS) data; census material; government information and contextual research findings. Also, this picture will be added to by official data – government information – and recent research focusing upon specific issues.

Leaving home, leaving care and homelessness

> Make sure you're on your feet first, make sure you're prepared and plan ahead. Don't leave on your 16th birthday just because you can. (Advice from Scottish care leaver to other young people in care, in Dixon and Stein, 2002)

Young people leave care to live independently at a much earlier age than other young people leave home.

Moving on, which utilised a quasi-experimental design, found that in both the survey of 183 young people and follow-up sample of 74 young people, nearly two-thirds left care before they were 18 and just under a third did so at just 16. This contrasts with 87 per cent of a similar age group who were living at home (Biehal et al, 1995).

In *Still a bairn?*, a Scottish survey of 107 young people and follow-up sample of 61 young people, nearly three-quarters of those who legally left care or moved to independence did so at 15 (21 per cent) or 16 (52 per cent). The average age at which young people in the study made the transition from care was 16, and the great majority (94 per cent) moved on from care before their 18th birthday. This contrasted with a model age of 22 for males and 20 for females. A significant minority of young people in this study (40 per cent) felt that they had not had a choice about when they moved on from care (Dixon and Stein, 2002; 2003).

In these two studies the main reasons for leaving care young included young people's expectations, wanting to be independent, 'I was 17, I felt as though I needed to move on with my life.' Some young people also left care following a placement breakdown, often when they were 16 or 17 and there were few other placement options. The age structure, culture and expectations of, and within, children's homes also led to young people leaving care early − young people seeing themselves as 'out of place' and 'pushed out' at 16. Finally, the scarcity and costs of foster care placements meant that some young people were unable to remain in foster care, 'I was too old and the foster carers wanted younger kids.' (Young people's views, in Dixon and Stein, 2002)

In a study of young people leaving foster care Sinclair and colleagues (2003) found that living independently at 16 and 17 was often as a result of young people not being able to settle either in foster care or at the family home. However, foster carers recognised that young people did need ongoing support into adulthood, although this was not always acknowledged by social services who wanted them to move on to independence before the carers thought they were prepared and ready to leave (Fry, 1992; Schofield, 2001; Sinclair et al, 2003). It is not only foster carers who are critical of leaving care early. In *Still a bairn?* the main message from young people who had left care to other young people was, 'don't leave too soon coz it won't be easy…', 'Don't leave on your 16th birthday just because you can' (Dixon and Stein, 2002).

In summary, whereas the current trend for a majority of young people in the general population is for extended transitions − by staying on in education and remaining dependent, to varying degrees, upon their families well into their 20s − many care leavers have to make accelerated transitions and thus shoulder adult householder responsibilities at a much earlier age than other young people (Joseph Rowntree Foundation, 2002). What are their accommodation pathways after they leave care?

In *Moving on*, both the survey and follow-up samples identified a pattern of initial moves to transitional forms of accommodation, such as hostels, lodgings and stays with friends, for just under half of the group. For some of these young people who were not ready for independent accommodation this proved to be helpful preparation. In the follow-up sample a fifth moved to independent tenancies in the public, voluntary or private sectors when they first left care and this figure rose to nearly 60 per cent 18–24 months later. Most of these young people needed ongoing support to sustain their tenancies. For many, their first two years out of care were marked by movement, with over half making two or more moves and a sixth making five or more moves, including planned moves.

In *Still a bairn?* most young people surveyed (61 per cent) had moved three or more times since leaving care, and around a quarter of young people in the follow-up sample had moved two or more times in the previous six months. In research carried out in Northern Ireland, *Meeting the challenge?*, 91 young people leaving care were surveyed and 41 followed-up. Nearly two-thirds of the young people had initially returned home from care, but within six months less than half were still living at home (Pinkerton and McCrae, 1999). In an Irish study, *Left out on their own*, (a survey of 166 young people leaving care and a follow-up case study analysis of 60), a third of the young people who had returned home had moved into other forms of accommodation and a similar proportion had moved from other forms of accommodation back to live with their families six months after leaving care. Nearly two-thirds had moved once, and just under a quarter three or more times, within six months of leaving care (Kelleher et al, 2000).

Most of the young people in these studies experienced further movement after leaving care and some had a more chaotic housing pathway, including periods of homelessness. In Scotland, 40 per cent of the young people surveyed reported having experienced homelessness since leaving care, and this compared with 20 per cent of young people in the English and Northern Irish research and 16 per cent of young people in Ireland.

The *London* research, based upon interviews with a representative sample of young people from eight London boroughs, carried out since the introduction of the Children (Leaving Care) Act, presents a more positive picture of accommodation patterns. Following the introduction of the Act in October 2001, 53 young people were interviewed between April and March 2002 and 44 of these young people were interviewed again between March and July 2003. At the time of the first interviews

11.2 per cent could be said to be in 'unsuitable accommodation' (hostel, b&b, homeless). By the second interview only one young person fell into this category and almost 90 per cent responded that they were happy where they lived. This included young people living in semi-independent accommodation (just under a quarter at both interviews), young people living independently (increased from 43.4 per cent to just over a half) and young people living with their foster carers (from four to five young people). Two-thirds of the young people remained in their accommodation between the two interviews, while a quarter moved on to independent living (Hai and Williams, 2004).

The findings from retrospective studies of young adults who have been in care at some time in their lives, spending time at hostels for homeless people, varies from between just under a third to nearly two-thirds (Randall, 1988; 1989; Strathdee, 1992; McCluskey, 1994; Strathdee and Johnson, 1994). Craig, who compared homeless and non-homeless young people, found that those who were homeless were 10 times more likely to have spent time in statutory care during childhood (Craig, 1996). Also a number of studies show that care leavers may be at particular risk of sleeping rough. Between a quarter and third of rough sleepers were once in care and *The Big Issue* found that nearly one in five vendors had been in care (Anderson and Quilgars, 1995; Strathdee and Johnson, 1994; Kirby, 1994; Markey, 1998; SEU, 1998; *The Big Issue*, 2001).

However, it is important to note the differences in the homelessness rates between follow-up and retrospective studies, the former, with the exception of Scotland, recording lower rates than the latter – but in both types of study, care leavers would be over-represented compared to the general youth population.

Education

> I feel that if I'd stuck in at school, if I'd got the right education at the right blooming time, I could have really gone further … I'm angry at other folk … for not pushing me in my education. (Scottish care leaver, in Dixon and Stein, 2002)

Young people leaving care have lower levels of educational attainment and post-16 participation rates in education, than young people in the general population.

In the *Moving on* survey sample two-thirds had no qualifications at all, only 15 per cent had a GCSE (A–C grade) or its equivalent, and only one young person gained an A level pass. The qualitative sample revealed a similar pattern. Those who did gain some qualifications were overwhelmingly female (85 per cent) and from fostering backgrounds (70 per cent). The differences are striking in comparison with data from both national and participating local area school attainment tables. Nationally for the relevant year, 38 per cent, and locally, 30 per cent, attained five or more GCSE passes at grade A–C. As regards A levels, 25 per cent of boys and 29 per cent of girls attained at least one pass.

In the *Still a bairn?* survey almost two-thirds of young people had no standard grade qualifications compared to the national average of seven standard grades. Only 3 per cent had Highers compared to 30 per cent of the general population of school leavers (Dixon and Stein, 2002). In the Irish and Northern Irish studies, half of the young people left school with no qualifications at all, again a far greater proportion than for young people in the general population (Kelleher et al, 2000; Pinkerton and McCrae, 1999).

These findings in respect of educational attainment are also supported by other research studies from the UK, United States, Ireland, Canada and Australia (Festinger, 1983; Raychuba, 1987; Jackson, 1989–1990; Jackson, 1994; Jackson, 2001; Heath et al, 1989; Aldgate et al, 1993; Cook, 1994; Cashmore and Paxman, 1996; Stein, 1994; Stein et al, 2000; Kufeldt et al, 2003).

Analysis of data from the National Child Development Study (NCDS), a cohort study of 17,773 children born between 3 and 9 March 1958, and followed up in 1965, 1969, 1974, 1981 and 1991, reveals lower levels of educational attainment among cohort members who had experienced care, compared to those who had never been in care (Cheung and Heath, 1994):

> Perhaps the most striking percentages are those for respondents with no qualifications. Of the people (aged 23) who had been in care 43 per cent had no qualifications compared with only 16 per cent of their peers who had never been in care. In a society in which qualifications are of major importance for success in the labour market, the educational disadvantage suffered by children in care hardly needs emphasising. (Cheung and Heath, 1994, p365)

More specifically, when respondents who had been in care secured qualifications, they tended to be lower level ones. Whereas two-thirds of their peers secured qualifications at O level or above, only one-third of the respondents who had been in care achieved an equivalent number of passes.

The NCDS data was also analysed to include divisions within the 'care' category. This pointed to two main conclusions. Firstly, respondents who were only briefly in care were not disadvantaged in terms of educational attainment or subsequent educational or occupational status compared to non-care respondents. Secondly, the most disadvantaged group were those who came into care before 11 years of age and typically remained in care for around nine years. They not only had low educational attainment, but also had even lower occupational attainments than would have been expected given their level of qualifications.

The NCDS data was further analysed to consider the effects of social origin on the findings. Is it possible that children who have been in care come from particularly disadvantaged backgrounds, and that the findings simply indicate that poverty leads to a cycle of disadvantage? When controlling for social origin, however, this explanation was not supported. The study concluded that, 'the legacy of care cannot be explained purely as a legacy of poverty' (Cheung and Heath, 1994, p371).

On a more positive note, government performance data for England shows that the percentage of care leavers with at least one qualification (one GCSE or GNVQ pass at any grade) has steadily risen from 31 per cent in 1999–2000, to 37 per cent in 2000–2001 and to 41 per cent in 2001–2002 with girls performing consistently better than boys – as in the national trend. However, where comparable data is available in 2000–2001, the 37 per cent for looked-after young people contrasts with 95 per cent for all Year 11 young people. Also, when comparisons are made for A*–C grades, in 2001–2002, just 8 per cent of young people in Year 11 who had spent at least one year in care gained five or more GCSEs, compared with half of all young people. In the same year almost half had no qualifications at GCSE level. Of Year 11 pupils who had been in care for one year or more, 42 per cent did not sit GCSEs or GNVQs, compared to just 4 per cent of all children (SEU, 2003).

Also, progress towards meeting government targets shows that just under one in four authorities met the target of half of care leavers obtaining one GCSE or GNVQ in 2001; and only 38 per cent met the target for improved educational, employment and training outcomes at age 19 in 2002.

In school, looked-after children also do less well than other children in Key Stage tests. In 2001–2002, in Key Stage 1 (age 7) looked-after children achieved at just under 60 per cent of the level of other children, at Key Stage 2 (age 11) just over 50 per cent, and at Key Stage 3 (age 14) 33 per cent, as well as their peers (Department of Health, 2003).

Post-16 careers: education, employment, training and benefits

> I think I am special because I tried and finished college. (Care leaver, in Dixon and Stein, 2002)

Educational disadvantage casts a long shadow. Care leavers are more likely to be unemployed than other young people aged 16–19.

In *Moving on*, 36.5 per cent of the survey sample and 50 per cent of the qualitative sample were unemployed compared to a mean of 19 per cent for other young people. In the follow-up sample, half of the young people were unemployed within a few months of leaving care and nearly two-thirds failed to establish a stable career pattern during the course of the research, facing periods of short-term casual work, interspersed with episodes of training and unemployment.

In the Scottish survey, *Still a bairn?*, at the time of leaving, over half of the young people were unemployed, a quarter were still in education or training and a tenth were in paid work. But nearly two-thirds of young people in the follow-up study had failed to find stable employment, education or training by the end of the follow-up period (Dixon and Stein, 2002).

In the Irish and Northern Irish follow-up samples a third and a quarter of young people respectively were unemployed (Stein et al, 2000). Also, research into a small sample (36) of young people leaving care in a predominantly rural area found that within a year a third of young people were unemployed, a quarter were employed. Seventeen per cent were in training, 14 per cent were in education, and 11 per cent were full-time carers (Allen, 2003).

Analysis of the NCDS data adds to this picture. This revealed that respondents in 1981 and 1991 who had been in care were much more likely to be unemployed, were more likely to be in semi-skilled or unskilled manual work, and were less likely to be in managerial work than their peers who had never been in care. Through statistical modelling of the data, Cheung and Heath suggest that respondents who had been in care in 1981 and 1991 fared less well than would have been expected:

These results suggest that unqualified respondents who had been in care were more likely to be unemployed or, if employed, were more likely to be restricted to low skilled manual work than were the unqualified respondents who had never been in care. In this respect there does appear to be a continuing legacy of care. Respondents who had been in care suffered an additional penalty when they entered the labour market over and above the penalty that they suffered in the educational sphere. (Cheung and Heath, 1994, p369)

Surveys carried out in 1998 and 2002–2003 by Broad – before and after the Children (Leaving Care) Act 2000 – provide evidence of recent changes in England. The 1998 survey of leaving care projects working with 2,905 young people showed that 11 per cent of the total sample were working full time; 27.5 per cent were participating in youth training, further or higher education; 4 per cent were in part-time work; and just over a half were unemployed – two and a half times the unemployment rate for this age range (Broad, 1998).

During 2002–2003, the same author collected data from 52 leaving care projects working with 6,953 young people. As regards education, employment and training (data on 4,304 young people), 14 per cent were employed full time, 31 per cent were in further/higher education, 29 per cent were unemployed, 8 per cent were in training, 6 per cent were not working on medical grounds and 4 per cent were employed part time (Broad, 2003).

The most significant change between 1998 and 2002–2003 was the increase of young people in further education, from 17.5 per cent to 31 per cent and the related proportion of young people not in any employment – a reduction from just over 50 per cent in 1998 to 29.5 per cent in 2002–2003.

In Hai and Williams's *London* study, also carried out since the introduction of the Children (Leaving Care) Act, at the time of the first interviews with young people, just under 19 per cent were unemployed, under two-thirds were in education (50.9 per cent) or training (11.3 per cent) and almost one in five were unemployed (19 per cent). However, by the second interviews those not in education, employment or training had increased to 30 per cent, with a 20 per cent drop in those in education (Hai and Williams, 2004).

Performance evidence data from England for 2001–2002 shows that 46 per cent of care leavers (with whom local authorities were in touch) at age 19 were in education, training or employment compared with 86 per cent of all young people aged 19 in the population as a whole (Department of Health, 2003). There is also evidence that young people seeking asylum have higher levels of participation in education (40 per cent) and higher education (10 per cent) at age 19 than other care leavers, where only 23 per cent were in any form of education. Only 14 per cent of asylum-seeking young people were not in any form of education, training or employment at age 19 compared to just under a third of all care leavers (Department for Education and Science, 2003). Also, it is estimated that only 1 per cent of care leavers go on to university compared to 37 per cent of young people living with their birth families. Higher education outcomes are discussed in Chapter 5 (Jackson et al, 2003).

The impact of poor educational attainment leaves many care leavers ill-prepared for an increasingly competitive youth labour market. The research findings and government data presented above consistently reveal higher levels of unemployment and lower levels of participation in post-16 education, employment and training – although as discussed above, there is recent evidence of greater involvement in further education since the introduction of the Children (Leaving Care) Act. However, these findings still mean that between a third and half of young care leavers are not in education, employment or training and are dependent on financial support. Many of these young people are living at, or near, the poverty line, and are struggling to survive and to make ends meet.

Specific groups of care leavers

Young parents and parenthood

> She just makes my life … and I enjoy that responsibility and I'm glad that I'm a parent.
> (Young parent, in Biehal et al, 1995)

Another area of contrast between care leavers and other young people is in relation to teenage pregnancy and early parenthood.

In *Moving on*, one quarter of the young women in the survey sample and one half of young women in the follow-up sample were coping with early parenthood, being aged between 16 and 19 when their babies were born. Another study found that one in seven young people were pregnant or had children at the point of legal discharge from care (Garnett, 1992). These patterns contrast sharply with those for the population as a whole. For the comparable year, only 5 per cent of young women aged 15–19 had children and only 2.8 per cent were lone mothers at 19 years of age. The average age for maternity at that time was 26.5 years, and recent research suggests that this age is increasing – indicating another difference in transitions to adulthood between care leavers and other young people (Kiernan and Wicks, 1990).

In *Still a bairn?* just over 20 per cent had a child (13.6 per cent) or were either themselves or had a partner who was pregnant (6.8 per cent) within 5–24 months after moving on from care. This contrasted with the 6.7 per cent of young women in the 16–19 age group living in Scotland who experience pregnancy (NHS Scotland, 2000). A similar proportion, 20 per cent, in the Northern Irish research, *Meeting the challenge*, had a child, were pregnant, or were responsible for pregnancy, six months after leaving care.

A study of inter-generational transmission of social exclusion estimates that young people who have been in care are two and a half times more likely to become adolescent parents than other young people (Hobcraft, 1998), and data from the British cohort study indicates that children of women who have spent time in care themselves are two and a half times more likely to go into care than their peers (Cheesbrough, 2002).

However, despite re-occurring panics about teenage parenthood, and especially lone mothers being seen as social problems, this is not inevitable. Research has also drawn attention to the social context in which mothering takes place, the financial dependence it entails, and, where young mothers had sufficient supports, especially from their mothers, their ability to cope and provide good quality care for their children (Sharpe, 1987; Phoenix, 1991). There is also evidence from young mothers who had been in care of a feeling of maturity and status, thus contributing to achieving an adult identity. The gains for some included a renewal of family links, and improved relationships with their mothers and their partners' families (Biehal and Wade, 1996). Hutson found that young mothers in supported accommodation tended to experience less poverty and reduced social isolation (Hutson, 1997). However, too often young mothers who have been in care had inadequate or no support after they have left care (Corlyon and McGuire, 1997).

Reasons for early parenthood are less well researched. In the *Moving on* study, just over half of the parents said that their pregnancies were unplanned, and nearly two-thirds of these were 17 years or younger. In *Still a bairn?* just over a quarter of the young people in the survey sample that had a child had become a parent at 15, while over half had become a parent at 16 years old. Just under half of the young people who had a child described themselves as a 'lone parent' while over a half said that their child did not live with them.

Disruption through movement in care, problems with truancy and the absence of a consistent carer capable of inspiring trust may mean they miss out on advice. As Biehal and colleagues, remarked:

> Safe sex requires an ability to communicate between partners and where young women have had poor chances for developing trust, confidence and a positive identity, relating to young men in a confident and assertive way can be difficult. (Biehal et al, 1995, p132)

Research based on the views of 63 young people, including 47 young women and 16 young fathers, all of whom had become, or were about to become parents for the first time, and 78 professionals and carers, adds to this picture (Chase et al, 2003a; 2003b). This research suggests that early pregnancy should be seen in the context of young people's pre-care and care experiences, including their feelings of isolation, rejection and loneliness, their difficulties in trusting people and services, and their vulnerability to a range of problems, such as drugs, alcohol, exploitation, violence and homelessness.

Many of the young people interviewed described experiences of care that had introduced them to early sexual activity and experimentation with drugs and alcohol, as well as disrupted educational experiences resulting in leaving school at an early age.

These young people repeatedly reported having very limited access to information and support about sexual health and relationships issues, often as a result of: missing school or poor-quality sex and relationship education at school; the failure or inability of foster carers and residential workers to address these issues; negative or unsupportive attitudes of care workers; and poor communication particularly when young people experienced some form of learning disability. Many of these young people described learning about sex education on their own (Chase et al, 2003a and 2003b).

The research also found that 90 per cent of young people interviewed reported no or only sporadic use of contraception at the time they became pregnant with their first child. The remaining 10 per cent said that their contraception failed. Less than half the young people said that they had received any kind of support in helping them make a decision about the pregnancy and most described being put under pressure by professionals, carers or birth parents to have an abortion – which most young people were strongly against (Chase et al, 2003b).

As suggested above by Hutson, for the majority of young women and men in Chase's sample, becoming a parent was a very positive event. However, they faced a range of difficulties including financial difficulties; accessing some services; feeling that social workers were interested in their care and protection of the child, thus creating barriers to support; inadequate housing; coping with parenthood as well as leaving care; and the lack of awareness of the needs of young fathers in helping to bring up their children (Chase et al, 2003b).

Haydon's qualitative research, based upon focus group discussions with 23 young parents, echoes many of these findings, especially in regard to the focus on abortion and child protection concerns by professionals, financial hardship, the variation in support available, and difficulties experienced by young parents in continuing in education (Haydon, 2003).

Young black and minority ethnic care leavers

I just class myself as myself really, I'm not saying that I'm white, I'm not saying that I'm black. I just say, 'Look, I'm mixed race and I'm proud of it.' (Care leaver, in Biehal et al, 1995)

Just under a quarter of young people looked after in England aged 16 or over are from minority ethnic groups (Department for Education and Skills, 2004). However, there are very few studies that have been able to make significant comparisons between black and white young people, or are solely of black and minority ethnic young people leaving care. An early study with an exclusive focus on this group found that trans-cultural placements, or placements in predominantly white areas, could leave black young people with subsequent confusion about their cultural identity. A lack of cultural knowledge affected their confidence and self-esteem, and was an additional burden at the time of leaving care (First Key, 1987; Black and In Care, 1984). Ince's small qualitative study of 10 black care leavers has also highlighted identity problems derived from a lack of contact with family and community as well as the impact of racism and direct and indirect discrimination upon their lives after leaving care (Ince, 1998; 1999).

Consistent with other findings, by far the largest group of black and minority ethnic young people (black, Asian, mixed heritage) in both the *Moving on* survey and qualitative study were young people of mixed heritage (Bebbington and Miles, 1989; Rowe et al, 1989; Garnett, 1992). Black and minority ethnic young people tended to enter substitute care earlier and stay longer than white young people (Barn, 1993; Barn et al, 1997). However, apart from this factor, there was very little difference between their care careers and those of white young people. After leaving care they had similar housing and employment careers, although they were slightly more likely to make good educational progress after leaving care than white young people. The majority of these young people had experienced racist harassment and abuse.

In *Moving on*, young people's definitions of their ethnic identity were often complex, varied and shifted over time (Tizard and Phoenix, 1993; Hall, 1992; Owusu-Bempah, 1994). Their identification with a particular ethnic group was strongly related to young people's identification with or rejection of family members. Close family links, integration within the local black community, placements with black carers and reinforcement by parents or peers generally contributed to a positive sense of black identity. But some of the mixed heritage young people felt that black or white people did not accept them – although they could feel secure about their identity.

Research in progress based upon a quantitative sample of 261 care leavers, including 116 (45 per cent) from a minority ethnic background, from six English local author-ities, will contribute to a greater understanding of ethnicity and leaving care (Barn et al, 2004). Just over half of the sample (55 per cent) was white. Of the origins of young people from a minority ethnic background, just over a third (35 per cent) were of mixed heritage, just under a third were Caribbean (30 per cent), a quarter were African and just 10 per cent were Asian.

There were many similarities between the experiences of white young people and those from minority ethnic backgrounds. But white young people were likely to leave care earlier than mixed parentage and Caribbean young people, and there is some evidence in the study that placements with black families may protect young people from minority ethnic backgrounds against further placement instability. Caribbean, mixed heritage and white young people were more likely to be excluded from school than African and Asian young people. Preliminary findings also include concerns about racism expressed by minority ethnic young people (Barn et al, 2004).

Refugee and asylum-seeking young people

All you want to do is do well and make everybody proud of you. This includes your parents even though they are not here. (Fawzia, aged 19, Kidane, 2002)

Since completing my 1997 report, *What works in leaving care?* a major change in the child welfare population has been in the increase in the numbers of unaccompanied asylum-seeking and refugee children in the UK, who are either looked after or supported by local authorities. In the year ending 2002, 1,050 unaccompanied asylum seekers aged 16–17 were looked after, representing 11 per cent of all 16- and 17-year-olds who are looked after. It is estimated that 7 per cent of all care leavers in England are asylum seekers (Department for Education and Science, 2003). However, the total number of unaccompanied children and young people supported by English local authorities either seeking asylum or who had been granted refugee status or exceptional leave to stay is much larger. In January 2001 a mapping exercise carried out by the British Agencies for Adoption and Fostering (BAAF) and the Refugee Council found 6,078 young people within these groups. Most of these young people are 16- or 17-year-olds and young men (BAAF and Refugee Council, 2001).

The exile of many of these children and young people may be a consequence of parental death or their inability to care for them due to war, or different forms of persecution – for example, being forcefully recruited into military service, being made to denote family or group members, having to undergo compulsory re-education or the prohibition of their religious or political beliefs. Against this background they may have high levels of both emotional and material needs but also demonstrate resilience (Kidane, 2002; Kohli and Mather, 2003).

There has been very limited research into the specific needs of this group but that which has been carried out often reveals a failure to respond to their needs. Many of these young people experience difficulties in accessing mainstream education, bullying and racial harassment. They may also be placed in poor accommodation (Dennis, 2002). An Audit Commission survey found that refugee children and young people were routinely being supported in temporary accommodation – over half of young people over 16 and 12 per cent of those under 16 being placed in bed and breakfast accommodation. The survey also found that many local authorities did not offer these young people a full needs assessment and only one-third had individual care plans. A Barnardo's survey also highlighted the large number of unaccompanied young asylum seekers living in unsuitable accommodation (Audit Commission, 2000; Barnardo's, 2000).

There is also evidence of variability in local authorities' interpretations of their duties under the Children Act 1989 (Mitchell, 2003). Some local authorities are deciding not to 'look after' these young people, and instead are supporting them under Section 17 of the Children Act 1989 – thus avoiding their legal responsibilities under the Children (Leaving Care) Act to support them during their journey to adulthood (Aycotte and Williamson 2001). However, this is likely to change as a result of new Guidance (Department of Health, 2003b) and a legal challenge in the High Court, which ruled that they should be supported under the Children (Leaving Care) Act (Prasad, 2003).

Young disabled people

> Where do I go from here? I haven't got a clue what it's about or anything really, no infor-
> mation on it at all … I'd like to know what rights I've got now I'm nearly eighteen … that
> isn't clear at the moment. (Young disabled care leaver, in Rabiee et al, 2001)

There has been very little research into the experiences of young disabled people leaving care even though they are over-represented amongst those 'looked after' by local authorities (Rabiee et al, 2001). Priestley and colleagues argue that there is 'almost no cross fertilisation of knowledge' between the literature on leaving care and disability (Priestley et al, 2003). For many young people leaving the parental home is a key marker of adulthood and in terms of their housing aspirations young disabled people are similar to their non-disabled peers. Most want to leave the parental home (Dean, 2003).

A survey of young disabled people in the general population, which included a comparison sample of non-disabled peers, estimated that up to 40 per cent 'find great difficulty in attaining independence in adult life comparable to that of young people in the general population' (Hirst and Baldwin, 1994, p110). The study showed that disabled young people were less likely than their non-disabled peers to be living independently of their parents and to be in paid employment, and were more likely to be dependent on benefits, have lower incomes, have lower self-esteem, and have more restricted social lives (Hirst and Baldwin, 1994). The literature has also highlighted the problems young disabled people face in accessing housing, moving away from parents, being involved in leisure activities and finding employment (Morris, 1995; 1998; 1999).

In *Moving on* 13 per cent (23) of the survey sample were disabled young people. The largest group, over half, was comprised of young people who had been classified as emotionally or behaviourally disturbed, four had severe learning disabilities, three a physical disability and two had a mental health problem. Compared to other young people in the survey sample they had fewer educational qualifications, were more likely to be unemployed and were over-represented among the homeless.

The most recent research into the experiences of young disabled care leavers identifies the problems they experience in their transitions to adulthood. In *Whatever next?* Rabiee, Priestley and Knowles gathered data on 131 young disabled people, including a qualitative sample of 28 young people. In the local area 197 young disabled people under the age of 18 were identified as looked after, representing a third of all young people with disabilities and complex health needs receiving social services (Rabiee et al, 2001; Harris et al, 2002).

At the outset, the study described the segregation of young disabled people from mainstream childcare services within social services. It also detailed the great difficulty the researchers had in identifying young disabled people who were looked after in the research population area.

The research also showed that for many of these young people there was a lack of planning, inadequate information and poor consultation with them. Young disabled people who did not have parents to argue on their behalf, or whose parents were not familiar with the system, were often disadvantaged in accessing the information needed to help them in making choices as they approached adulthood. Friends also often provided advocacy and support. Transitions from care for these young disabled people could be abrupt or delayed by restricted housing and employment options, and inadequate support after care.

The range of accommodation options was often determined by vacancies in existing adult services, rather than by the needs or wishes of young people. For young people with 'mild' or 'moderate' learning difficulties there was a lack of support for independent living and young people with 'multiple' impairments were more likely to move into residential care (Rabiee et al, 2001). For example, Dawn, an 18-year-old, was living in a residential home for older people and Nathan at 15 was living in a children's short-break unit. The study also identified the gap between mainstream and specialist services that offered little middle ground for young people, particularly those with learning difficulties that were able to live independently if given adequate support.

As regards education the study uncovered young people who had 'fallen out' of mainstream education as well as the failure for other young people, in specialist provision, to distinguish between education and social care which impacted upon their employment prospects. Young people with committed parental advocates were more likely to obtain their preferred choice of school or college and less likely to be placed in non-educational day care alternatives.

In respect of independence skills the study stressed the need to link skills development with real life situations, avoid the low expectations often associated with impairment and care, and link skills with housing, transport, education and the use of money, rather than making them isolated technical or instructional issues. The researchers comment:

> Independence should never be equated with doing things 'on your own'. Such measures will always devalue the independence of young people who use help to perform daily tasks. Making choices and exercising control over how things are done is a more significant measure of independence. (Rabiee et al, 2001, p58)

The study also identified gaps in transitional planning resulting in abrupt transitions – including a loss in continuity in support and young people feeling lost, undervalued or pushed to make a move before they are ready. Other problems identified in the study included lack of consultation and involvement of young people, lack of collaboration between specialist and mainstream leaving care services, and other relevant agencies such as health, education and careers. Young people valued support from parents, relatives and former carers, which also had implications for transitional planning in the balance between formal and informal support (Priestley et al, 2003).

In the *London* research young disabled people were described as 'a hidden group within the project.' The specialist leaving care teams had difficulty in identifying young disabled people to be part of the research sample, 'reflecting the lack of engagement by the teams with this group of looked-after young people.' Young disabled people were more likely to be dealt with by specialist disabled teams and may not be accessing mainstream services (Hai and Williams, 2004).

Young people with mental health problems

Looked-after young people

Children and young people who are looked after are subject to many of the major risk factors associated with the development of mental health problems. Indeed, there is a close link between the risk factors associated with the likelihood of coming into care and the development of psychiatric disorders: lone and young parenthood; reconstituted families; severe marital distress; low income; overcrowding or large family size; paternal criminality; and maternal psychiatric disorder (Rutter, 1995; Garmzey, 1987; Bebbington and Miles, 1989; Melzer et al, 2000; Koprowska and Stein, 2000).

However, very few UK research studies have been carried out using comparison groups, to establish the prevalence of mental disorder in looked-after young people. In Oxfordshire, McCann and colleagues (1996) found that 57 per cent of young people living in foster care and 96 per cent of those in residential care had some form of psychiatric disorder: a combined total of 67 per cent. The comparison group of young people living with their families had a rate of 15 per cent. The percentages of looked-after young people with conduct disorder (28 per cent) over-anxious disorder (26 per cent), major depressive disorder (23 per cent) and psychotic disorder (8 per cent) was significantly higher than in the comparison group (0 per cent; 3 per cent; 3 per cent and 0 per cent, respectively). In relation to the care population the authors concluded 'that a significant number of adolescents were suffering from severe, potentially treatable psychiatric disorders which had gone undetected' (McCann et al, 1996).

Since McCann and colleagues' study, the Office of National Statistics (ONS) have carried out two national surveys of the mental health of young people in England (Melzer et al, 2000; 2003). The first survey, carried out in 1999, obtained information about the mental health of 10,500 young people living in private households. The second survey focused on the prevalence of mental health problems among young people aged 5–17 who were looked after on 31 March 2001. A total sample of 2,500 within the age group was drawn, approximately 1 in 18 of all looked-after children and young people. The two surveys allowed for comparisons to be made between the two samples.

The older age group, the 11–15-year-olds – who were most likely to become care leavers – were four to five times more likely to have a mental disorder compared with the private household sample: 49 per cent compared with 11 per cent (there was no comparative data on 16–17-year-olds as they were not included in the private household survey). The rates for each broad category of disorder were: emotional disorders: 12 per cent compared with 6 per cent; conduct disorders: 40 per cent compared with 6 per cent; hyperkinetic disorders: 7 per cent compared with 1 per cent.

As regards gender, in the 11–15 age group, the proportions of young people with any mental disorder were 55 per cent for boys and 43 per cent for girls; for the 16–17-year-olds the rate for both groups was around 40 per cent. At 16–17, girls had a higher prevalence of emotional disorders and a lower rate of conduct disorders than boys.

In terms of placements, two-thirds of young people living in residential care were assessed as having a mental disorder, compared with half of those living independently, and about 40 per cent of those placed with foster carers or with their birth parents. The distribution of all mental disorders was significantly different according to placement. Children living with their birth parents or in residential care were about twice as likely as those in foster care to have emotional disorders. Children living in residential care were far more likely than those in foster care or living with their birth families to have conduct disorders. The prevalence of mental disorders tended to decrease with the length of time in their current placement.

The survey also established a close association between mental disorders and physical complaints compared with those young people who had no mental disorder. Also children and young people with a mental disorder were nearly twice as likely as children with no disorder to have marked difficulties with reading (37 per cent compared with 19 per cent); mathematics (35 per cent compared with 20 per cent); and spelling (41 per cent compared with 24 per cent). Over a third (35 per cent) of children with a mental disorder were three or more years behind their intellectual development, twice the rate of that among children with no disorder. Among the children with a mental disorder 42 per cent had a statement of special educational needs (SEN), twice the proportion found among the sample with no mental disorder. There was an association between having a mental disorder and truancy. Finally, the survey also showed that young people with a mental disorder were much more likely to smoke, be regular drinkers and use drugs than children with no disorders.

Research has also identified high levels of behavioural and emotional disturbance among young people referred to social services. Triseliotis and colleagues (1995) found that the behaviour of 90 per cent of young people was rated above the 'normal' cut-off point using an adaptation of the Rutter scale (thus allowing comparisons with the general population). In another study, over three-quarters of young people referred for assessment were thought by professionals to be displaying disturbed or disturbing behaviour. The highest levels of disturbed behaviour were to be found among those young people living in residential care (Sinclair et al, 1995). A study of young people who go missing from substitute care also found that young people with emotional and behavioural difficulties were over-represented among those who went missing often, and were at risk of detachment from safe adult networks (Wade et al, 1998).

Care leavers

A study of 48 care leavers found that 17 per cent had long-term mental illnesses or disorders, including depression, eating disorders and phobias, but this represented nearly all the females (87 per cent) within the sample. Just over a third of the total sample had deliberately self-harmed since the age of 15 or 16, either by cutting, over-dosing, burning, or a combination of two or more of these. Nearly two-thirds of the young people had thought about taking their own lives and 40 per cent had tried to when aged between 15 and 18, at the time they were leaving care (West, 1995; Saunders and Broad, 1997).

There is also evidence that mental health problems may increase over time for care leavers. In *Still a bairn?* there was a fourfold increase in young people reporting mental health problems up to 11 months after leaving care (Dixon and Stein, 2002).

Adults who have been in care or adopted

Studies of adults adopted, fostered or living in residential care, or some combination of different leaving arrangements, also contribute to our understanding of mental health problems (Koprowska and Stein, 2000).

Triseliotis and Russell (1984) compared adoptees with children brought up in residential care. The two groups differed in a number of ways at the outset; principally, the adoptees had spent less time with their family of origin, entering both the care system and their final placement at an earlier age, and coming more frequently from younger mothers who were single. Before final placement, more of the adoptive children had 'moderate to severe emotional problems' and three were referred for psychiatric help, in contrast to none of the residential children. By the time they left school, however, the situation had reversed, with a significantly higher proportion of the residential children showing emotional and behavioural problems and being referred for psychiatric help. The adopted children had happier memories of their upbringing, and described more benign and less punitive regimes than the residential group. Both groups improved upon the living circumstances of their family of origin, but there was a difference between those coming from 'very "disturbed" backgrounds'. The adoptees did as well as those from less disturbed families, while the residential group did not. These were the people who were likely to have psychiatric problems. While the study concluded that social disadvantage was not transmitted from one generation to the next, it showed that, through a complex interplay of factors, those brought up in residential care were disadvantaged.

Quinton and colleagues (1984) compared women brought up in institutions for extended periods, and women brought up in their family of origin. Overall, nearly a third of the women from institutions showed good parenting in contrast to almost half of the comparison group. However, 40 per cent of them showed poor parenting, in contrast to only 11 per cent of the comparison group. Nearly a third of the women brought up in institutions had a psychiatric disorder, and a quarter had personality disorders (5 per cent and 0 per cent in the comparison group, respectively). Even so, a fifth of the women from institutions had a good overall outcome; Quinton's team noted that the most important protective was a stable relationship with a 'non-deviant' husband or partner.

Cheung and Buchanan (1997), and Dumaret and colleagues (1997) examined the psychosocial adjustment of adults who had been in care. They used very different methods: Cheung and Buchanan re-analysed results from two 'sweeps' of the National Child Development Study, at ages 23 and 33, while Dumaret and colleagues interviewed adults who had been fostered. Cheung and Buchanan compared people who had been in care with people who had experienced 'severe social disadvantage' and people who had not experienced 'severe social disadvantage'. They used the Malaise Inventory, which indicates a tendency towards depression. Those who had been in care had a risk of higher scores, but there were significant gender differences. Women in each group were at risk for higher scores than men in the same group, but the risk for all women lessened as they grew older. It increased for men who had been in care. Although they offer some tentative suggestions about why these changes occurred, more research is required to understand them. Dumaret's team found a more positive picture than Quinton's. More than half of their respondents were 'well integrated', and 68 per cent were well integrated or average. Their sample consisted of young people brought up in foster care rather than institutions and they had received specialist support from a dedicated fostering agency.

Rowe and colleagues (1989) researched the psychosocial development of young people living in long-term foster care across a broad range. Many of the children had problems when they joined the foster family. The most common problems reported by foster carers were attention-seeking behaviour or being withdrawn, sleeping difficulties, temper tantrums and lack of concentration. During placement, only six children had no problems. The most commonly reported problems were lack of concentration and temper tantrums, with anti-social behaviour being more common than 'neurotic' symptoms. Boys were more prone to problems than girls. There were 37 black children in the study, all of whom were fostered with white families. There were no differences in adjustment between black and minority ethnic and white children.

St Clair and Osborn (1987) and Stein (E) and colleagues (1994) also considered children currently in care, but Stein (E) and his team were primarily interested in prevalence of psychiatric disorder, while St Clair and Osborn looked at educational and behavioural outcomes. Stein (E) and colleagues found that the girls in care had significantly higher rates of 'externalising' behaviour than the girls in the community sample; their scores were equal to those of the boys in care. In the community sample, the boys' scores were higher than the girls'. Many of the young people, especially the boys, show developmental delays.

Physical health

There has also been limited research into the physical health of care leavers. The 2001 ONS survey discussed above (Melzer et al, 2003), also surveyed the general health of looked-after young people. Two-thirds of all looked-after children and young people were reported to have at last one physical complaint including: eye and/or sight problems (16 per cent); speech or language problems (14 per cent); bedwetting (13 per cent); difficulty with co-ordination (10 per cent); and asthma (10 per cent).

Also, analysis of data from the *Looking after children: assessment and action* records (Department of Health 1991a) reveals high levels of general unmet health needs.

Over half of the sample were identified as having health or behavioural needs (Ward and Skuse, 2001). The Who Cares? Trust survey of 2,000 young people looked after in England found that 40 per cent under the age of 11 felt that they had not received enough information about their development (Shaw, 1998). In relation to leaving care, in *Still a bairn?* 12 per cent of the young people surveyed reported having a long-term physical health problem, while almost a fifth (18.7 per cent) reported having other health problems, such as asthma, eczema, hearing impairments or problems associated with drug or alcohol misuse (Dixon and Stein, 2002). Broad and Saunders also identify the health problems of young people leaving care: just under half of their sample of 48 young people had long-term health problems. The young people surveyed felt that their health was affected by housing, personal relationships, their care experience, as well as 'depression' and their general feeling about life (Saunders and Broad, 1997). Two Scottish studies, one of young people living in a variety of residential settings and the other of young people living in foster care placements, found that the young people living in foster care reported themselves as being happier, healthier, eating better, exercising more, and being far less likely to use drugs than their counterparts in residential care (Ridley and McCluskey 2003; Scottish Health Feedback 2001; 2003).

Drug use among young people in, and leaving care

> It was stopping me from functioning properly during the daytime because I was either asleep or ill from the come down of the drugs. (Young man, 29, in Ward et al, 2003)

Having been neglected for many years, drug consumption by young people in care and during their transition to adulthood has been explored in two recent studies (Newburn et al, 2002; Ward et al, 2003).

The first study was based upon a survey of 400 young people (average age 15.4 years old), living in residential and foster care, life history interviews with 35 of those young people, and individual interviews and focus groups with care staff.

This study found that compared with the general population, young people in care have relatively high levels of illicit drug use, much higher proportions having used cannabis, solvents, amphetamines, ecstasy and cocaine. There was significantly higher use of crack and heroin among young people in care than in the general population and also more regular use of cannabis, cocaine, crack and heroin. The same study also found that young people had often started using drugs early, which is correlated with problem drug-taking. However, drinking alcohol was a relatively infrequent activity. Many of the young people had experienced loss, bereavement and rejection and some of these young people had turned to drugs to compensate for these negative experiences and to combat depression (Newburn et al, 2002).

The second study surveyed 200 young people (average age 18 years old) in the process of leaving care or home early, or having recently left care, and followed this up with interviews of a sub sample of 30 young people.

This study also found high levels of self-reported drug use compared with general population surveys. But this was mainly cannabis use. Almost three-quarters (73 per cent) have smoked it, one half (52 per cent) in the last month, and a third (34 per cent) reporting that they smoked daily. Fifteen per cent had used ecstasy and one-tenth had used cocaine within the last month. Little difference was found in drug use between young men and young women but young black people were less likely to use drugs (44 per cent had not taken any drug) compared with 82 per cent of young white people who had. Among those of mixed parentage, 95 per cent had taken an illicit drug at some point in their lives. Two-thirds of the sample reported that they were daily cigarette smokers and one-third drank alcohol at least once a week.

Except for two groups, the qualitative interviews showed that lower levels of drug consumption were reported as young people assumed or approached independent living status. The groups that were exceptions to this were those who went to live in hostels, and those whose movement to independent living was premature or poorly planned. Parenthood and practical responsibilities, such as household management, when well planned as part of the care-leaving transition, encourage more stable lifestyles and reduce levels of drug use. The study also found that 'maturing out' of drug use occurs at a younger age for care leavers than that found within the general population (Ward et al, 2003).

Offending

Official data on the offending rates of looked-after children in England were collected for the first time in 2000. The figures showed that looked-after young people were three times more likely to be cautioned or convicted of an offence than their peers (Department of Health, 2003c).

In their study of children's homes, Sinclair and Gibbs (1998) found that 40 per cent of young people with no cautions or convictions had one after six months of living in a children's home. Research by Taylor (2003) suggests that for those who had already been involved in offending, care often had a negative effect, escalating the criminal behaviour of young men.

Care leavers are over-represented in custodial institutions, although caution should be exercised given that existing data is derived in the main from retrospective estimates – including young people who may have spent any time from one night upwards in care! Earlier estimates of the percentages of adult and young prisoners who have been in care at some time in their lives suggest just under a quarter (23 per cent) and over a third (38 per cent) respectively (Prison Reform Trust, 1991). More recently, Hazel and colleagues found that 41 per cent of children in custody had at some time in their lives been in care (Hazel et al, 2002). However, the relationship between care, offending and custody is complex and under-researched.

The transition to adulthood of youth 'aging out' of the foster care system in the United States

The main body of research discussed above is derived from research studies carried out in the United Kingdom with some reference to other European studies. This picture of the problems and challenges faced by young people leaving care is collaborated by Courtney and Hughes's review of the literature on the 'young adult outcomes of former foster youth' in the United States (Courtney and Hughes, 2003). The studies selected included those to which comparative regional and national data had been applied by another reviewer (McDonald et al, 1996) as well as Courtney and colleagues' own research (Courtney et al, 2001).

There is a consistency of findings in relation to housing instability, including periods of homelessness. When they are discharged from care many young people have to leave their last out-of-home care living arrangement and they are less likely to be able to live at the family home than other young people.

As discussed above, young people are also likely to have deficits in educational attainment and low rates of participation in further 'college' education, higher unemployment rates and dependency on public assistance, 'their mean earnings were well below the federal poverty level for up to two years after leaving out-of-home care … they earn on average too little to escape poverty' (Courtney and Hughes, 2003).

Also, consistent with the findings discussed above, former foster young people suffer from more mental health problems than other young people. This includes evidence of higher rates of seeking help, admission to psychiatric facilities and higher levels of depression. Courtney and colleagues (2001), whose subjects completed a standardised self-report mental health assessment found that the overall psychological health of the young adults was significantly worse than that of their peers of the same age and race.

Former foster young people have a higher rate of involvement with the criminal justice system, including the likelihood of a criminal record and adult imprisonment, than the general population. However, an issue not explored in the UK literature is victimisation. Courtney and colleagues asked subjects whether they had experienced any form of victimisation since they had left care. A quarter of young men and 15 per cent of young women reported that they had experienced some kind of serious physical victimisation involving being 'beat up, choked, strangled or smothered, attacked with a weapon or tied up, held down, or blindfolded against their will'. Also, 11 per cent of young women reported having been sexually assaulted, 10 per cent that they had been forced against their will to engage in oral or anal intercourse. Altogether, 13 per cent of young women reported having been sexually assaulted and/or raped within 12 months of discharge from care.

As regards family links, most of the studies reviewed found that 'at least monthly' contact between former foster young people and their mothers ranged from one-third to one-half of respondents, and with fathers from one-quarter to one-third of respondents. Courtney and colleagues found 80 per cent of former foster young people with at least one sibling to have visited a sibling at least once since discharge from out-of-home care. The same study also found that a majority of former foster young people maintain ongoing contact with their former foster families.

In their study of young people who aged out of care in Wisconsin, Courtney and colleagues (2001) found that over half of the young people (56 per cent males and 54 per cent females) experienced one or more of the following outcomes within 12–18 months of leaving foster care: reliance on public assistance, homelessness, incarceration, serious physical victimisation, sexual assault, or rape.

Key messages

- The findings from early leaving care studies were, in the main, small, exploratory user-opinion and non-experimental studies. As such, they provided much-needed descriptions and insights into the lives of young people leaving care. But their size, scope and design limitations left important questions unanswered – in particular, how the needs of care leavers compared to other 'non-care' young people. Studies from 1990 onwards are presented which address this question.

- The evidence from these studies shows that young people leaving care have to cope with the challenges and responsibilities of major changes in their lives – in leaving foster and residential care and setting up home, in leaving school and entering the world of work or, more likely, being unemployed and surviving on benefits, and in being parents – at a far younger age than other young people. In short, many have compressed and accelerated transitions to adulthood.

- During this journey to adulthood they are more likely than other young people to become young householders, be homeless, have poorer qualifications, lower levels of participation in post-16 education and higher levels of unemployment.

- Young parents, although pleased to be parents, often lacked personal and financial support.

- Black and minority ethnic young people may face identity problems due to being isolated from their families and communities, as well as racism.

- Refugee and asylum-seeking young people may receive poorer accommodation and educational services than other looked-after young people and be excluded from statutory support after leaving care.

- Some young disabled people's transitions from care may be delayed or be more abrupt than other care leavers' – poor planning, inadequate information and consultation, and a lack of co-ordination between agencies may restrict their opportunities during their transition to adulthood. They may also be denied access to mainstream leaving care services.

- There is also evidence that looked-after young people, those leaving care, and adults who had been in care were likely to experience mental health problems.

- Care leavers also have higher levels of drug use than other young people.

- A review of research literature from the United States corroborates many of these findings in respect of young people who 'age out' of foster care.

4 Leaving care services

This chapter is concerned with leaving care services. Researching services is often referred to in jargon as 'process evaluation'. Such evaluations may include descriptions of the range of services provided, the type of work undertaken and the classification of services. Process evaluations are derived from different types of research methods, including observation, analysis of project data, records and case files, as well as interviews and focus-group discussions with key stakeholders.

The historical context of leaving care provision from the Children Act 1948 to the Children (Leaving Care) Act 2000 has been documented in Chapter 2. This chapter will draw upon some of that historical material as well as research findings to explore the development of leaving care services and the different approaches to their classification.

The development of leaving care schemes

The introduction of services for care leavers carrying the label 'leaving care' is of recent origin. Maureen Stone, in her 1989 survey of 33 specialist schemes, found that only one was in existence in 1978 and the majority, 82 per cent, started in 1985 or later (Stone, 1990). But the designation 'leaving care' does not mark the beginning of leaving care services any more than, say, the introduction of 'community homes' by the Children and Young Persons Act 1969 marked the start of residential childcare. Schemes, projects and programmes to assist young people leaving care are as old as the childcare services themselves, whether they were unrecognised as part of the ordinary and informal responsibilities of foster carers, or more organised, such as the early work placement schemes pioneered by Barnardo.

As Chapter 2 details, following the introduction of the Children's Departments in 1948, 'working boys' hostels', 'mother and baby homes', lodging houses and designated probation and aftercare and childcare officers to assist young people leaving care were provided in many local areas – to name some of the more prominent initiatives. However, as also detailed in Chapter 2, the reorganisation of the personal social services and the introduction of the Children and Young Persons Act in 1971, led to a decline of specialist aftercare work in many local authorities. The new generic all-purpose social workers, the high priority given to child protection work and the community focus of radical social work contributed to the neglect of care leavers and their aftercare. Also, discretionary welfare embodied in the new care orders led to a lowering of the age at which young people left care.

During the 1980s, against a wider background of major economic and social change – contributing to high levels of unemployment, a shortage of housing and reductions in social security – the desperation of many of these young people, some homeless and destitute, was highlighted. Campaigning organisations, including Shelter, researchers, practitioners working with young people, and, not least, young care leavers themselves, all made their voices heard. This led to the introduction in some areas of specialist leaving care schemes, as well as providing the momentum for change to existing legislation to assist care leavers.

The development of specialist schemes was seen by social services as a way of meeting their leaving care responsibilities under the Children Act 1989. Research carried out between 1990 and 1995 showed that they provided a focused response to the core needs of care leavers – for accommodation, personal and social support, finance and help with careers (Biehal et al, 1995). Their work, post-Children Act 1989, included:

- a contribution to policy development and the co-ordination of leaving care services within local areas
- developing a flexible range of resource options for young people, and, in some instances, co-ordinating access to them, especially in relation to further and higher education, employment and training, housing and financial support
- developing inter-agency links to ensure an integrated approach to assisting young people
- providing advice, information and direct individual and group-based personal support to young people, including those preparing for leaving care and those living independently in the community
- providing training and consultancy services for staff and carers
- monitoring and evaluating their services.

Broad's 1996 English survey of 46 specialist leaving care projects working with 3,308 young people found that the majority, nearly two-thirds, started after the Children Act 1989 was enacted. In his sample, just under a third of these projects was provided and funded entirely by local authorities, just over a third provided by voluntary organisations but funded from a range of different sources, and a third jointly funded by local authorities and voluntary organisations (Broad, 1998; 1999).

Specialist leaving care teams and projects continue to play a major role in the delivery of leaving care services in England and Wales, and Scotland. Broad, in his 2002–2003 survey, was able to identify 300 leaving care teams working in England and Wales (Broad, 2003).

Broad surveyed 52 of these leaving care teams working with 6,953 young people, describing the work of one in six English and Welsh local authorities. Local authorities provided three-quarters of the teams; the remaining quarter was split almost evenly between teams run solely by voluntary organisations and those jointly provided by local authorities and voluntary organisations. In comparison with his 1998 profile, this shows significantly more local authority and less voluntary and joint providers, and although it is not possible to identify general trends from these samples it may well be that there is a greater role for local authorities in the implementation of the Children (Leaving Care) Act 2000. The survey found that nearly two-thirds of the teams were established before the introduction of the Act, including half of them before 1995. Just over a quarter were established in anticipation of, or immediately after, the introduction of the Act.

The survey found that the 52 teams employed 595 staff, the equivalent of a ratio of 12 young people to 1 staff member, compared to a 15:1 ratio in the 1998 survey. A quarter of the staff were identified as 'specialist staff who are personal advisers' under the Children (Leaving Care) Act, and just under half as 'specialist leaving care social workers'. The remaining staff were 'other specialist' and this included education and employment workers (11.1 per cent) and health staff (2.1 per cent).

The main work of the teams surveyed included assistance with education, employment and training, accommodation, health and financial support. In addition, teams identified work with specific groups of young people including young disabled people, unaccompanied asylum-seeking young people, and young people on remand. The leaving care teams also identified their anti-discriminatory practice and their work in supporting post-16 placements. Finally, they provided information on their work as personal advisers including needs assessment and pathway planning (Broad, 2003).

The *London* research into the implementation of the first two years of the Children

(Leaving Care) Act in eight London boroughs identifies significant changes in the structures, policies and resources of leaving care services during this period (Hai and Williams, 2004).

First of all, this included the development of specialist 16-plus leaving care services in seven of the areas, with workers having full case management responsibility for eligible, relevant and former relevant young people, case responsibility passing to the team in the young person's 16th year. In the remaining authority the leaving and aftercare service was contracted out to an external voluntary agency.

A second major change was the greater involvement of staff from other agencies, either located within the team, or attached to them in a named capacity. This included staff from Connexions, health and mental health, housing, education, drugs services, children's rights, psychology, family mediation, nursing, benefits, outreach, befriending and mentoring. On the basis of interviews with staff and young people the research found that these arrangements allowed the social workers with case responsibility to concentrate on the statutory requirements of the Act while the specialists were able to co-ordinate their agency response, such as housing, education and health.

Third, ring-fenced money had resulted in both better resourcing of services, including increased staffing levels, and greater financial freedom to meet the needs of young people, especially to respond to crises and problems. Overall, the study saw the Act as contributing to the increased profile of leaving care services within the authorities (Hai and Williams, 2004). However, services were not seen as improving for all care leavers. Young disabled people were described as a 'hidden group among care leavers'. They were likely to be dealt with by specialist disabilities teams and be denied access to mainstream leaving care services – reflecting the division in services, and their underlying narratives, identified by Priestley and colleagues (2003).

In Scotland, Stein and Dixon's policy survey of all local authorities (response rate of 97 per cent) carried out during 2000 revealed that just over two-thirds of authorities had a specialist team or specialist staff with direct responsibility for providing throughcare and aftercare services. Just under 60 per cent of those teams were centrally located and nearly three-quarters were managed and funded by the social work department. The remaining specialist teams included those jointly managed and funded by the social work departments and the voluntary sector or other external agencies. All of these were centrally located. The centrally organised specialist team was the main specialist model – there was no evidence of dispersed specialist staff within fieldwork teams. Just over a half of these teams or specialist staff provided a service to all eligible young people within their authorities, the others provided services for young people not able to live at or to return home. Over half reported having a written description of the services provided by the team (Dixon and Stein, 2002).

Just under a third of social work departments had no specialist team or staff with direct responsibility for providing throughcare and aftercare services. Most of these departments responded that field social workers, residential social workers and foster carers were involved in providing these services. However, most respondents were unable to identify the numbers of staff involved and less than half had a written description of the range of throughcare and aftercare services provided. Generally, non-specialist services were being provided in larger rural areas, or in geographical areas where the numbers of young people eligible to receive formal throughcare and aftercare were smaller (Dixon and Stein, 2002).

Classifying leaving care services

The classification of specialist leaving care services has been applied to individual schemes and projects as well as models of authority-wide provision, or both.

Different schemes were identified in the early literature by service delivery and philosophy (Stein, 1991). Service delivery models included: non-specialist service provision by mainstream childcare social workers, which, the results of a 1992 survey indicate, was the main form of provision at that time; specialist leaving care teams; supported accommodation projects; and youth and community work approaches (First Key, 1992a).

The main differences in philosophy and linked programme content identified in the early literature was between independence and inter-dependence models. The rationale of independence schemes was that young people should be trained to manage on their own from the age of 16 onwards through instruction in practical survival skills – 'domestic combat courses' – and by coping with minimum support. In contrast, inter-dependence models saw leaving care more as a psychosocial transition; a high priority being placed on interpersonal skills, developing self-esteem and confidence, and receiving ongoing support after a young person leaves care (Stein and Carey, 1986).

In their in-depth study of four leaving care schemes, Biehal and colleagues suggest a three-dimensional basis for classifying scheme distinctiveness (Biehal et al, 1995).

First, how do schemes compare in their approaches to service delivery, in terms of perspective, methods of working and the extent to which their work is young person demand led or social work planned? Second, how do schemes compare in terms of the nature of the providing agency, whether statutory or voluntary, including its culture and organisational, management and staffing structures? Third, what contribution do specialist schemes make to the development of leaving care policy within their local areas?

The results of a 1999 English survey of best practice in leaving care (based on responses from 42 local authorities) suggest that despite the diversity of service types, four main models of authority-wide provision were common at that time (Stein and Wade, 2000):

- a 'non-specialist service', where responsibility for delivering a service rests primarily with field social workers, sometimes in collaboration with carers
- a 'centrally organised specialist service', consisting of a centrally organised team of leaving care workers providing an authority-wide service, primarily to care leavers
- a 'dispersed specialist service', where individual specialist leaving care workers are attached to area-based fieldwork teams
- a 'centrally organised integrated service': an emerging model that attempts to provide an integrated service for a wider range of vulnerable young people 'in need', such as homeless young people, young offenders and young disabled people. Integration is facilitated through a multi-agency management and staffing model.

A survey of the 33 London boroughs adds to this picture (Vernon, 2000). Vernon's research identified two different types of specialist teams.

First of all, a specialist dual-system arrangement, which entailed the young person being referred to the specialist team, but with statutory responsibility being retained by the locality social worker. The leaving care specialists would provide the preparation and aftercare support, 'without the disadvantage of the "authority" tag, seen to be associated with statutory responsibilities'. Most of these teams were located in their own premises and moving on to one was seen as part of the 'rite de passage' for the young person – and this was reflected in the name of the projects, for example, the Independence Plus Project and the Young Person's Independence Service.

Second, looked-after adolescent teams, which acquired statutory responsibility for the young person and, in the main, worked with young people from the age of 15 upwards. The rationale for the setting up of these teams was to attract staff who enjoyed, and had a commitment to, working with adolescents and to prevent the delay of cross referral built into the system described above.

The London survey also cited contractual arrangements with voluntary service providers and teams for vulnerable young people – the integrated service model – identified in the best practice service above.

Drawing upon the research completed since the Children (Leaving Care) Act suggests the emergence of what could be described as a 'corporate parenting case model'. Its main features are, firstly, case responsibility held by the designated personal adviser. This could be seen as an extension of legal authority in respect of qualifying young people under the Act – against the background of the failures of permissive legislation. Secondly, the increased role played by other agencies – a shift from more informal links to formal agreements – as specified in the needs assessment and pathway planning requirements (Broad, 2003; Hai and Williams, 2004; Dixon et al, 2004).

In addition to the main models of authority-wide provision there is a very wide range of projects, many provided by the voluntary sector, which provide services for care leavers or wider groups of vulnerable young people including care leavers – although, as suggested above, they are increasingly incorporated into local leaving care services through formal agreements. *Care leaving strategies: a good practice handbook* (Department of Health/Centrepoint, 2002) describes a range of these projects and initiatives and categorises them around: improving preparation; providing an appropriate range of accommodation; tailoring individual support; accessing education, training and employment; improving the participation of care leavers; providing clear information for care leavers; and monitoring, evaluation and future planning (see Chapter 6 for a discussion of some of the practice examples given).

United States: leaving care services

In the United States, congressional concern about the extent to which older foster young people were prepared to manage their lives after care led to the passage of the Independent Living Initiatives, Public Law 99-2272, Comprehensive Omnibus Reconciliation Act 1985 (Mech, 1994). This law authorised funds for states to establish and carry out programmes to assist young people aged 16 and older to make the transition to independent living, leading to the development of a national network of schemes. In 1993, the federal independent living programme attained permanent status as an entitlement securing an annual budget allocation ($70 million in 1994). Most recently, the Foster Care Independence Act 1999 (Public Law 106-9) gives states more funding and greater flexibility in providing support for young people making the transition to independent living (Courtney and Hughes, 2003).

As regards classification of services, Courtney and Terao (2002) provide a descriptive typology which categorises them into life training skills, mentoring programmes, transitional housing, health and behavioural health services, educational services and employment services.

However, as Courtney and Hughes point out, focusing on the range of services may detract from common programme elements including: case management; their underlying philosophy – many adopt a youth development philosophy which emphasises opportunities for young people to contribute to their community, increase their personal confidence, and provide guidance to other young people; and that many are provided as one part of a wider range of services (Courtney and Hughes, 2003).

Courtney and Hughes also point to the limitation in the categorisation of services in excluding the variation in local policies – for example, in allowing young people to remain in care longer or providing financial support for college education.

Key messages

- Designated 'leaving care' schemes had, in the main, been introduced since the mid-1980s – although as Chapter 2 documents, specialist leaving care services go back much further in time. A case of rediscovery rather than innovation!
- Specialist schemes have been developed to respond to the core needs of care leavers for accommodation, personal and social support, finance and help with careers.

- There is no single model or blueprint for leaving care schemes. Process evaluations in the UK suggest there are differences in terms of philosophy, service delivery, the culture of the providing agency and in their contribution to policy development.
- As distinct from individual leaving care schemes, models of authority-wide provision include: non-specialist; central or dispersed specialist; and integrated provision for vulnerable young people.
- The introduction of the Children (Leaving) Care Act 2000 has led to the development in England of a 'corporate parenting case model' in some areas, better resourcing and, overall, to the increased profile of leaving care services.
- There is evidence that young disabled people leaving care are not accessing mainstream services.
- There is also a wide range of projects aimed at assisting either care leavers or other vulnerable young people including care leavers. There is a similar range of project provision in the United States although no classification of state-wide provision.

5 The outcomes of leaving care services

This book began by posing the question 'what works for young people leaving care?' So far the building blocks have been an outline of the historical context, an exploration of the problems and challenges faced by young people leaving care and a description of the different types of leaving care services. But what makes a difference to the lives of young people leaving care?

Attempts to evaluate the impact of leaving care services on subsequent outcomes are still at an early stage in the leaving care field, as they were when I wrote my original report in 1997. Indeed, I cited Ed Mech, the principal United States researcher at that time, who wrote in 1994 that the absence of such research, including RCTs, was 'the Achilles' heel of the independent living enterprise' (Mech, 1994, p142; Mech and Rycraft, 1995). In a similar vain, Courtney and Hughes, researchers who are currently carrying the leaving care torch in the United States, writing in 2003, comment, 'the new focus on outcomes monitoring and program evaluation is welcome … and provides hope that the field may be guided in the future by more than "practice wisdom" alone' (Courtney and Hughes, 2003, p39).

Of course it is not an easy task to establish whether young people who participate in the, purely hypothetical, Pudsey Independent Living Project achieve the desired outcomes, and are therefore different than they would have been if they had not participated at all. The growing literature on outcomes acknowledges the complexity of the task, given the range of contextual and interpersonal factors that help to structure the life chances of young people (Knapp, 1989; Parker et al, 1991; Cheetham et al, 1992; Sinclair, 2000; Shaw and Gould, 2001). However, despite the many influences it is fair to assume that planned interventions do have an impact, positive or negative, on what happens to care leavers and therefore there is a need for more outcome studies to evaluate the impact of leaving care services.

As stated in Chapter 1, in the past 20 years there have been no studies in this area that have adopted an experimental design. However, there have been a small number of follow-up outcome studies using quasi-experimental designs. What do they tell us about service outcomes for care leavers?

In addressing this question, this chapter will begin by exploring the findings in respect of specific outcome areas. This will include accommodation, education, post-16 careers, further and higher education, life skills and social networks and relationships. It will also consider a more holistic approach to measuring outcomes, as well as research from the United States evaluating whether or not outcomes are linked to general or more targeted services. It will then present the main findings from English and United States research following up young people leaving foster care placements. Finally, drawing upon these and other studies, it will propose different outcome groups for young people: a 'moving on' group; a 'survivors' group, and a 'victims' group.

Accommodation outcomes

In Chapter 3, I identified the compressed and accelerated transitions of many care leavers to independence compared to the extended transitions of young people leaving home. The chapter also explored the 'push' and 'pull' factors, and the difficulties for many young people in achieving stability in their accommodation and living arrangements after leaving care, including periods of homelessness (Biehal et al, 1995; Sinclair et al, 2003; Pinkerton and McCrea, 1999; Dixon and Stein, 2002; Kelleher et al, 2000). But how were these young people assisted and what difference did it make?

In the English and Scottish studies, specialist leaving care schemes and services played a major part in the 'moving on' process. This included planning transitions, preparing young people, providing follow-up support and meeting their accommodation needs. Accommodation services provided by schemes in these jurisdictions included directly managed accommodation in trainer flats or specialised hostels, floating support schemes, access to supported lodgings or hostels provided by other agencies, and arranging and supporting young people in independent tenancies.

In *Moving on* (Biehal et al, 1995), two types of housing outcomes were assessed. First, the type of accommodation obtained by the young person and second, the young person's ability to sustain a tenancy. Grading housing outcomes was based on an assessment of both the nature of the accommodation and the young people's and workers' views as to its acceptability for their current needs. Sustaining a tenancy involved an assessment of how the young person was coping with budgeting, and maintaining relations with landlords and neighbours.

During the period of 18–24 months after the young people began using leaving care schemes, there was an increase in the proportion of those whose accommodation was assessed as 'good' but no change in respect of the comparison group. Leaving care schemes were working with those young people who had the most unstable early housing careers and were able to help the vast majority of them find 'good' accommodation within two years of leaving care. Both groups showed a slight overall improvement in their ability to sustain a tenancy within two years of leaving care, but the most significant difference in this respect was gender. Young women were twice as likely to be good at sustaining a tenancy than young men, a greater proportion displaying an ability to budget and to maintain reasonable relationships with landlords, neighbours or other residents. Why this was so is an area requiring further research. A fruitful line of enquiry could be how far preparation for leaving care, while young people are living in foster and residential care, 'addresses gender-related differences in expectations, motivation and behaviour' and, perhaps, equally significantly, whether and how there is a transfer of learning after young men leave care. Young men behaving very badly have a lot to lose.

In *Still a bairn?* (Dixon and Stein, 2002) two accommodation outcome measures were used. Firstly, coping outcomes were measured by the worker's perception of how well the young person was managing in their accommodation. Secondly, 'housing outcomes' were based on a combination of hard data, such as the type of accommodation, and whether the young person considered it suitable.

On the first measure, two-thirds had good outcomes and a third poor outcomes six months after leaving care. On the second measure, just over half of the sample had good housing outcomes at the time of leaving care and six months later, although this included about 20 per cent of young people who had improved outcomes and a similar proportion whose outcomes deteriorated. There was no link between housing mobility and outcomes at six months; those who had unstable careers, including homelessness, generally moved to a more positive outcome at six months. There was a statistically significant relationship between good housing outcomes and poor family links, and young men were more likely to have good housing outcomes than young women. Also, young people who had good housing starting points were more likely to achieve good outcomes than those who had poor starting points.

These two studies highlight the positive contribution made by leaving care services in assisting young people with their accommodation needs, both at the outset and when they get into difficulties. Even for those young people experiencing the greatest instability, continuity of support by schemes often prevented a descent into homelessness or enabled a rapid escape from it. This was achieved in two ways. Firstly, by the role of schemes in increasing the range of accommodation options. Secondly, by the commitment and support from scheme workers in helping young people in sustaining their tenancies and being available to assist them at times of crisis.

Research in progress provides strong evidence of the association between stability in accommodation after young people leave care and positive outcomes in terms of employment, mental health and an enhanced sense of well-being, to some extent independently of young people's earlier care careers (Dixon et al, 2004). Assisting young people with accommodation can make a difference to their lives.

Education outcomes

As detailed in Chapter 3, a body of research studies and official data shows that many young people leaving care have poorer levels of educational attainment than their peers. What impact do leaving care schemes have upon education? What other factors are associated with good educational outcomes?

In *Moving on*, two aspects of educational outcome were assessed. Firstly, a measure of attainment to allow comparisons with the wider population of young people: good outcomes were defined as five or more GCSEs at grades A–C; fair outcomes as one to four GCSEs at grades A–C; and poor outcomes as low grades only or none. Secondly, in recognition of the poor attainment of looked-after young people, progress they made after leaving care was also included, assessed qualitatively from the interviews with young people, scheme workers and social workers: good outcomes meant attendance at school or college, or the young person or profession-al perceives they have made progress; poor outcomes, the young person attending school or college was unable to sustain attendance, or the young person or profes-sional perceives that no progress has been made.

Educational attainment at the point of leaving care was poor for both the young people participating in the schemes and for the comparison group of young people, and as detailed in Chapter 3 both groups fared much worse than the general popula-tion. There was also very little improvement in patterns of attainment for either group by the end of the study, as very few (15 per cent) continued their education after leaving care.

In *Still a bairn?* educational attainment was assessed according to the number of standard grades young people had achieved at the time of leaving care. Good outcomes were assigned to those gaining seven or more grades, fair outcomes to those achieving one to six grades and poor outcomes indicated no standard grades. On these criteria over half of the sample had poor outcomes, over a third fair outcomes and only 12.7 per cent good outcomes.

If specialist leaving care schemes and services had little impact upon educational outcomes, what did? In *Moving on*, the great majority of young people who gained some qualifications were female (85 per cent), in stable placements where they felt well supported and encouraged to achieve at school. All but one of the young people were in foster care and over half were in placements of more than six years, and the remainder in placements of between one and six years. In *Still a bairn?* those who achieved good educational outcomes had experienced stability, having had two moves or less during their last care episode (Biehal et al, 1995; Dixon and Stein, 2002).

There is also evidence that some young people who had several placements can achieve educational success if they remain at the same school (Jackson and Thomas, 2001). Research in progress also supports these findings: coming into care before the age of 14; spending longer in care; placement stability; and foster care placements were all associated with better outcomes (Dixon et al, 2004).

What works in achieving successful educational outcomes is placement stability over a longer period of time, living in foster care, and continuity of care and schooling in the context of a supportive and encouraging environment for study. Educational initiatives aimed at assisting looked-after young people are outlined in Chapter 6.

Post-16 career paths and outcomes

Again, as Chapter 3 has demonstrated, care leavers were more likely to have unsettled early employment careers and be unemployed than other young people in the general population.

In *Moving on*, employment outcomes were derived from an Economic and Social Research Council (ESRC) study of 5,000 young people which identified the three principal career paths of 16–19-year-olds as the academic route (school, further or higher education), the work route (full-time employment, stable youth training) and the insecure route (unemployment, unstable youth training, casual work). The two former routes were graded as 'good' and the insecure route as 'poor' (Banks et al, 1992: their follow-up response rate averaged out at 60 per cent and 70 per cent for the older and younger cohorts respectively).

Young people using the leaving care schemes were more likely to have embarked on insecure career paths when they first left care than those in the comparison group. Two-thirds of the schemes group were either unemployed, dropping in and out of training or doing occasional casual work, whereas over half of those in the comparison group were on the work or academic routes at this stage. Across both groups just over half (52 per cent) were unemployed in the early months after leaving care. These outcomes were significantly worse than those for the general population of 16–19-year-olds, where in the comparable year 22 per cent of 16–19-year-old males and 16 per cent of 16–19-year-old females were unemployed. Stability of care careers, as indicated by no moves, and last placement in foster care were closely linked to secure career paths at the time of leaving care.

However, within two years of leaving care more young people in both groups had slipped to the insecure route, but a greater proportion of those in the comparison group had slipped from the secure route. All bar one of those on the insecure route were unemployed and all those with full-time parental responsibilities disappeared from either path, all having previously been on the insecure route.

The majority of young people from both the participating and comparison samples were living at, near or below the income support level – or poverty line – and thus developing arrangements to meet their financial needs was a central part of the schemes' work. This role included implementing local authorities' discretionary powers to provide leaving care grants, 'top-up' payments and education grants as well as advising young people in respect of community care grants, social fund loans, housing benefit and income support (including severe hardship payments, bridging allowances and maternity grants). In addition, voluntary schemes, being centre based, were able to provide 'hidden' support, such as occasional meals, help with transport, a warm place to go and even holidays.

The career outcomes for both groups of young people were poor and generally worse for those using schemes than in the comparison group. As the authors of *Moving on* comment:

This may be due in part to the young people's prior educational attainment, to their lack of confidence or motivation, to other difficulties in their lives which make it hard for them to focus on career options or to the limited opportunities available to young people in the labour market. Nevertheless, there is clearly scope for schemes to develop initiatives to assist young people in establishing themselves on secure career paths. (Biehal et al, 1995, p269)

In *Still a bairn?* good employment and career outcomes included being in employment, education or training, and voluntary work if undertaken in addition to either of the former. Poor outcomes included unemployment and voluntary work. The research found that there was very little difference in young people's employment and career outcomes at the time of leaving care and six months later. Just over a third had good outcomes and just over two-thirds had poor outcomes at both points in time – although there was a very slight increase in good outcomes (from 35.1 per cent to 38.9 per cent). There was not a clear association with educational attainment and employment outcomes.

In *Moving on*, those who achieved good post-16 employment, education and training outcomes shared the same characteristics as those achieving educational success: stable care careers; continuous patterns of schooling; foster care backgrounds; and encouragement by carers to achieve well.

In *Still a bairn?* what was common to those who had good outcomes was informal support (family links and social networks) and, for those lacking this, formal support by leaving care staff or social workers. In addition, qualitative analysis of a small sample of young people who continued and succeeded in post-16 education points to stable foster care placements, settling well at school and being supported in remaining in education, by being able to stay on in foster care after formally ceasing to be looked after, or being supported by a specialist leaving care team.

In terms of what works, both *Moving on* and *Still a bairn?* provide evidence for the key associations with good educational outcomes. In addition, the Scottish research identifies the importance of both informal and formal support after young people leave care.

Further and higher education

As outlined in Chapter 3, Broad's 1998 and 2002–2003 surveys show a significant increase in young people's involvement in further education, from 17.5 per cent to 31 per cent and a related proportion of young people 'not in any employment', from just over half in 1998 to just under a third in 2002–2003. It is estimated that as only 1 per cent of care leavers go on to study at university, most of this increase is in respect of further education. As Broad suggests, the increased participation in further education may well be due to the transfer of financial support to local authorities for qualifying young people under the Children (Leaving Care) Act 2000, including the financial incentives they are able to provide in respect of young people entering further education. It is too early to assess the impact this will have upon educational outcomes, but potentially the wide range of further educational courses on offer provides an opportunity to help care leavers overcome educational deficits.

Jackson and colleagues (2003) have carried out the first UK study of the experiences of a sample of young people going on to higher education. Based upon the first of three successive cohorts of care leavers entering university, *By degrees* explored 'what enabled this group of care leavers to achieve an educational level which, though unremarkable by ordinary standards, is far above the attainment of the vast majority of young people in our care' (p70). What then contributed to the positive educational outcomes of this group?

First, compared with other children in care they had a more stable care experience. Those that had changed placements several times had often stayed at the same school, 'which was not only beneficial to their educational progress but meant they could keep friends and contacts with helpful teachers' (p70).

Second, the birth parents of these young people themselves saw education as important. Many of the young people welcomed having contact with their families, who encouraged them educationally, even though they didn't want to live with them again.

Third, and identified as the most significant in young people's accounts, was a placement with a foster carer, often late in their care careers, who saw, 'promoting the young person's education as a central aspect of their task' (p70). Most of the young people attributed their success to the support and encouragement given by their foster carers, including, 'a clear expectation that they would be going onto university after leaving school or college' (p70). For these late-placed young people, their relationships with their foster carers could be very close, like their own family or more of a semi-professional service. Also, for some young people the foster home would evolve seamlessly into supported lodgings.

Most of the young people in the sample had gone on to university from a foster home (or re-designated supported lodgings placement). Those who studied for their A-levels while living independently had the greatest problems – having to cope with all the practicalities often while studying.

Jackson and colleagues (2003) conclude, 'These young people are moving towards independence at their own pace with a sense of achievement. They were glad to have left the care system behind while mostly retaining affectionate ties with their former foster carers. The majority are ambitious and hard working and looking forward confidently to the future. The contrast with the many thousands of young people who leave care with no qualifications and few prospects could hardly be more extreme' (p71).

Life skills outcomes

What difference does preparation in life skills make? In *Moving on* three life skill outcomes were assessed as either good, fair or poor: budgeting skills; negotiating skills – managing encounters with officials, landlords, employers; and practical skills – self-care, domestic skills, such as cooking, laundry and cleaning.

Nearly two-thirds of the group had good practical skills at the point of leaving care and there was at this stage little difference between the leaving care scheme users and the comparison group. By the end of the study there was a slight improvement for both groups. As for budgeting, less than half in both groups had good skills on leaving care and both groups improved within two years of leaving, the scheme users showing a slightly greater improvement. As regards negotiating skills, the comparison group were more likely to have good skills on leaving care but were less able to maintain these skills by the end of the study. In contrast, scheme users were more likely to maintain their skills. Most of the young people using schemes had some help with life skills, in either a group or an individual setting, including those young people who moved into staffed or dispersed hostels.

Overall, leaving care schemes worked well in this area of life skills. Scheme users were more likely to have improved their practical and budgeting skills, and to maintain their negotiating skills, than those in the comparison group.

Achieving good outcomes in life skills was also linked to age on leaving care – 17- and 18-year-old leavers have better outcomes than 16-year-olds – and gender – young women being twice as likely to possess good practical skills (Biehal et al, 1995).

In *Still a bairn?* 'preparation' outcomes were assessed at the time of leaving care and 'coping' outcomes six months later.

Preparation outcomes included: self care – skin and hair care, healthy eating, keeping fit; social life – hobbies, socialising, boy and girl friends; domestic skills – cooking, shopping, budgeting; and lifestyle – safe sex, alcohol, drugs and smoking. Coping skills were organised around two main areas: housekeeping – able to keep a clean home, able to do laundry, able to shop for food and other things and able to budget; and health and social life – able to make friends, able to eat healthily, able to follow hobbies and interests, able to keep fit.

The study found that 'preparation' was significantly related to 'coping' after care. Domestic tasks and lifestyle were the most important in terms of overall coping but it was also enhanced by social skills preparation. Young women generally felt better prepared for domestic tasks, reflecting traditional gender stereotyped roles. The analysis also showed no difference between those young people who had been looked after at home – on home supervision – and those who had been looked after away from home, either in terms of outcomes for preparation or coping, suggesting that the preparation undertaken by substitute carers and specialist leaving care workers was just as effective as that provided by birth parents and family (Dixon and Stein, 2002).

Both these studies show the value of life skills preparation in helping young people cope after leaving care. There is an association between good outcomes and age of leaving care and gender – suggesting the need for more effective interventions with young men. Practice examples are described in Chapter 6.

Social networks, relationships and identity outcomes

What difference did leaving care schemes make to how young people felt about themselves, their social networks and their relationships with family and friends?

In *Moving on* (Biehal et al, 1995), the point of leaving care was a time at which many young people were attempting to make sense of their pasts – to trace missing parents, to find continuity in their lives and a sense of belonging. They needed a 'story' of their lives that made sense, reduced their confusion about both how and why events had happened as they did and to provide a more secure platform for their futures in the adult world. The research findings suggest that those who had retained their family links, even where contact was not very positive, seemed better able to do this. Knowledge of their families, at a minimum, gave a greater symbolic certainty to their lives. Those who remained confused about their pasts found life out of care more difficult to manage – they lacked self-esteem, were less confident and assertive.

There was little perceived difference between the black and minority ethnic young people (including mixed heritage) and white young people in relation to their degree of self-esteem, knowledge of their background and general sense of purpose. For the mixed heritage young people their sense of ethnic identity changed over time and their identification with a particular group was strongly related to their identification with or rejection of family members.

Many of the young people had poor relationships with their families, which ruled out a return home. However, family links were very important to most of them, including links with brothers and sisters, grandparents and other members of their extended family. And during the course of the research nearly half of the young women in the sample had become parents themselves.

Further analysis of family relationships in *Moving on* by Biehal and Wade indicated that although less than a third of young people had positive supportive relationships with one or both parents during their transition from care, within 18–24 months of leaving there was a *rapprochement* between young people and their parents, so by the end of the period, one half had positive relationships (Biehal and Wade, 1996). Their analysis also revealed help from parents when young people got into difficulties with their accommodation as well as practical help and company, especially where young people settled in the same neighbourhood. However, the renewal of relationships could be a mixed blessing – sometimes helpful, at other times disappointing as past difficulties resurfaced. Over a quarter of young people either had no contact at all with family members or had very poor relationships with both their parents and their extended families:

> Relationships were characterised by conflict, a lack of interest by family members or only infrequent contact. Some young people saw their parents regularly but did not experience this contact as supportive; parents were either reluctant to see them, were uninterested in them or conflicts regularly occurred during visits. (Biehal and Wade, 1996, p433)

Leaving care schemes were playing only a minimal role in mediating between young people and their families, tending to view this as the social worker's responsibility. But this was not always the case, for fewer than one-third of the social workers were active in this area once the young person had moved on. When social workers became involved with young parents, whether as a result of childcare concerns or not, there was a pervasive tendency to focus on monitoring childcare and thus to switch their support from mother to child. In contrast, the schemes, when involved, were able to support the young mother in her own right. The schemes were active in helping young people develop friendship networks. Their specialist knowledge of local young people and leisure provision as well as the schemes' own groups and drop-in arrangements were highly valued by young people.

As the authors of *Moving on* suggest:

> The quality of social networks and the ability to make and sustain relationships are often closely inter-related. In addition, young people's self concept and self esteem may have been determined to some extent by the quality of their social networks and might be expected to have some impact on the nature of their relationship skills. (Biehal et al, 1995, p269)

An analysis of outcomes reveals the close connections between the three areas. At the time of leaving care only one-third of the scheme participants and two-fifths of the comparison group had good social networks, that is, those comprising both friends and family. The majority of the young people were socially isolated and almost entirely dependent on professionals for support. Within two years of leaving care the difference between the scheme users and the comparison groups was slightly smaller and there was a slight increase in the proportion of young people with good social networks.

Those with good networks generally had good relationship skills (that is they perceived themselves, and were perceived by their scheme workers and/or social workers as reasonably confident in making and sustaining relationships). Those with a secure sense of identity (reasonable self-esteem, knowledge of background, a sense of ethnic identity, some evidence of a general sense of purpose) also had good or fair social networks and good relationship skills, whereas the majority of those with an insecure sense of identity had poor social networks and poor relationship skills.

In *Moving on* it was difficult to assess the impact of schemes upon outcomes. The schemes played an important part in befriending socially isolated young people as well as helping young people develop their relationships with others, and encouraging some young people to become more assertive in their dealings with others, or in negotiating with their families to avoid a breakdown in relationships. Positive role models, images and resources assisted black and minority ethnic young people. Also, schemes had an important role to play in building young people's self esteem and motivation indirectly, through assisting them in other areas, for example, by sustaining a tenancy or a training placement. But perhaps the key to successful outcomes lay within young people having positive, supportive relationships with family members or former foster carers.

In *Still a bairn?* two outcome measures were used for exploring contact and support from family and friends. In respect of family support good outcomes involved having contact with a family member and describing that contact as sometimes or mostly helpful. Poor outcomes included having no contact or contact that was considered by the young person as unhelpful.

The majority of young people had good family links at the time of leaving care (85.5 per cent) and six months later (77 per cent). For most young people in the follow-up sample families appeared to be providing both emotional and practical support: they were able to rely on them for help with money, food parcels, advice, help with finding work and with finding or providing accommodation. Family support came from extended family members, especially where relationships with parents had broken down. As well as mothers – who were most often cited as the person young people would turn to if in need of help – brothers and sisters, aunts and grandparents were also identified.

For those young people living away from home there was evidence that they could achieve good outcomes in coping, accommodation and education, if they received continuing support from specialist leaving care workers, social workers or both these sources of support.

As regards young people's social networks, these were assessed by taking into account contact with friends, whether they had someone to talk to if they felt sad or depressed and the extent to which they experienced loneliness. A good outcome was achieved if a combination of the above factors suggested that the young person had a support network and rarely felt lonely, a fair outcome where a young person was either without close friends or someone to talk to and occasionally felt lonely, and a poor outcome was indicated by a lack of friends, support networks and loneliness.

The analysis revealed a very close relationship in the percentages of young people falling into the assessed outcome areas at both points in time: good (50.8 per cent and 54.1 per cent) fair (36.1 per cent and 34.4 per cent) and poor (13.1 per cent and 11.1 per cent). All those who had poor social networks had poor outcomes in coping with life skills and most of these young people felt unhappy, over a third felt unloved and over a half lacked confidence. All but one said that they had often felt confused and angry. As in *Moving on*, then, there was a close association between social isolation, low self-esteem and confidence.

In terms of what works, both these studies show a close relationship between young people's social networks, family links and how they viewed themselves. They could be helped by positive links with family members or former carers, and by ongoing support from leaving care workers or social workers.

From starting points to outcomes

As suggested at the beginning of this chapter, there is a wide and diverse range of influences upon outcomes, and this poses methodological challenges – the Pudsey question!

In *Moving on*, it is argued that whereas the assessment of specific outcomes may give an indication of scheme interventions in particular areas of work, it can only present a partial picture. A 'holistic case analysis approach' is needed which takes account of the varied 'starting points' of the individual young people as well as their social environment. A holistic approach defines overall outcomes for a young person, which are broadly good or broadly poor (Doyal and Gough, 1984).

The minimum requirements for broadly good outcomes were conceptualised in *Moving on* as being when a young person was in good accommodation, had a regular means of support (which may be a wage, benefit payment or education grant and may include subvention by a local authority), had some degree of self-esteem and some sense of control over their lives, or their self-esteem and ability to take control of their lives has increased within two years of leaving care. This assessment took account of whether young people expressed unhappiness with their current situation or felt positive about their lives.

In *Moving on*, assessed by these criteria, the schemes' achievements – against the odds – were impressive. Overall outcomes that were either broadly good, or represented positive progress relative to young people's starting points, were achieved with three-quarters of scheme users and the comparison group:

> Bearing in mind that the starting points for many of the scheme users set a low baseline for development, the broadly positive outcomes for a large majority of the young people indicates that schemes can make an effective contribution to help young people negotiate their transition from substitute care to living independently. (Biehal et al, 1995, p290)

It could be argued that defining outcomes in this way is very minimalist and thus sets lower expectations for young people leaving care than for other young people – the 'minimum' social work thinking which the development of the *Looking after children* (Department of Health, 1991a) materials was introduced to challenge. This is a danger, particularly if such an approach were to replace other outcome measures. But this is not the intention, which is more to give recognition to the complexity of a process, or a journey towards specific outcome measures.

Services and outcomes in the United States: general or specific?

There have been a number of different approaches to evaluating the impact of leaving care service in the United States.

First, whether, how and in what combination schemes provide 'hard' or 'soft' living skills (Hahn, 1994; Maluccio et al, 1990). Hard skills pertain to meeting specific independent living needs, such as employment, housing and home management. Soft skills focus more on the development of self-esteem and personal concerns – a similar distinction to independence and inter-dependence philosophies as discussed in Chapter 4. Second, the differences between categorical independent living services, which provide a broad, general life skills preparation programme to all young people and an integrated services model linking social casework with preparation (Waldinger and Furman, 1994).

Evaluations of these different approaches highlight the importance of assessment as a basis for the planning of services (Hahn, 1994), the failure of categorical programmes to address educational needs and birth and foster family links, and the success of the integrated model in young people gaining, 'emotional and practical readiness' (Waldinger and Furman, 1994, p2).

A second study from the United States compared 63 non-foster care adolescents with 42 adolescents placed in kinship care and 69 young people in non-relative foster care in terms of their readiness for independent living (Iglehart, 1995). Bivariate analysis of self-report data revealed that foster care and non-foster care young people are not significantly different in their perceptions of independent living skill levels, their type of employment and their perceived overall preparation for independent living. However, both groups of foster care young people were more likely to perform poorly at school, worry about their future, plan to work full-time and not expect to be financially supported by their carers. And the group in non-relative foster care did not expect to live with their foster carers. Iglehart suggests:

> foster care brings with it worry … and the perception that the adolescent has to rely on him/herself after emancipation … these perceptions appear to capture a general sense of isolation and an absence of social support … while independent living programs may offer skills and knowledge needed for successful emancipation, it is not clear to what extent, if any, these programs can combat isolation and provide social support. (Iglehart, 1995, p430)

In an earlier exploratory study the same author identified the significance of educational success, placement stability and work in contributing to readiness for independent living – and conversely, the negative consequences of mental health problems (Iglehart, 1994).

Another approach to outcomes is illustrated by the Westat evaluation of independent living services. The Westat research, carried out in the United States, evaluated the impact of independent living services upon outcomes, by comparing samples of young people who had received services with those who had not.

Eight outcomes were assessed, that is whether the young people: could maintain a job for over a year; were a cost to the community; had completed high school; were able to access health care; had a support network available to them; had an overall sense of well-being; had avoided early parenting; and could function independently, as measured by a combination of the seven previous areas.

The independent living services were identified by young people from a list of 23 skills which included: budgeting money, opening a bank account, balancing a chequebook, obtaining a credit card, buying a car, getting car insurance, getting health insurance, getting health care, family planning, preparing meals, choosing nutritious food, doing housekeeping, shopping, finding a job, finding educational opportunities, finding a place to live, obtaining legal help, locating community resources, making friends, setting and achieving goals, expressing feelings, expressing opinions and making decisions.

First, when measuring the effect on the eight outcomes by comparing young people who had received no skills training with those who had received any type of skills training, no significant relationship was found between skills training and outcomes, 'we found absolutely no differences between those kids who had received services, no matter what they were, and those who had received none' (Cook, 1994, p226).

A second measure was to collapse the 23 services into 12 categories to see if any one of these skill categories as a category itself made a difference to outcomes. And it was found that several different areas of skill training did produce positive effects on related outcomes:

> The important term here is related, in that the receipt of health skills training showed effects on obtaining health care, and the receipt of employment services resulted in the youth being less of a cost to the community. (Cook, 1994, p226)

Skill areas also had an effect on other outcomes, but no consistency was found in any single area's effect.

A third measure was to assess the impact of a group of five skill areas, simulating a programme of services. These areas were: money management skills; obtaining credit; consumer skills training; job skills training; and help in obtaining educational opportunities. The research found that these in combination produced positive effects on the overall ability to maintain a job, obtain health care, not be a cost to the community, overall satisfaction with life, and in the composite measure of self-sufficiency. In addition, the likelihood of achieving better outcomes when receiving training in one, two, three, or all of these areas was better than when not receiving training in these areas.

The more that skill areas were increased, the larger the effects. The magnitude of the effect of these five core skills varied, depending upon the specific characteristics of the young people and the outcome being assessed.

> Using a young woman with the typical characteristics of youth discharged from care as an example, we estimated that if she were not provided [with] any of the five skills, her likelihood of maintaining stable employment 3 years after discharge was 22%. However, as the number of skill areas provided increased, the young woman's likelihood of maintaining stable employment increased from 40% with one service to 90% with all five services. (Cook, 1994, p226)

However, the Westat research found that random increases in the number of skills taught did not in themselves lead to a greater likelihood of achieving better results for specific outcomes. For example, adding skills training in socialisation, home management or obtaining community resources did not increase the probability of being able to maintain a job for a year. For the best results, services needed to be targeted towards the outcomes that they were intended to improve, and they needed to be provided in combination.

Three assessed outcomes – early parenthood, change in educational status after discharge, and having a social network – were not significantly increased by skills training in the areas of education, socialisation and family planning.

The Westat study concludes:

> The findings from this study indicate that services work best when a set of particular services are targeted to meet specific goals. The provision of any services, or even a number of services that are not targeted toward specific outcomes, was not shown to be effective in providing the desired results. (Cook, 1994, p227)

Outcomes of young people leaving foster care in England and the United States

Sinclair and colleagues in *What happens to foster children?* (2003), a three-year follow-up study of 107 young people leaving foster care, including a sub-sample of young people aged 16–18-plus when followed up, used three measures of outcomes.

First, they asked both social workers and foster carers how well the young people were doing on their latest information about them. They could respond (1) very well (2) as well as could be expected and (3) not very well.

The second measure, the 'trouble score', was the number of troubles the young person said they had experienced in the previous six months. The list included: being lonely; being homeless; always being short of money; having debts; regularly drinking more than you should; having rows with your family; having had a bad experience with drugs; getting into trouble with the police; being unemployed; living in a frightening area; getting into trouble at school; being bullied; falling out with an important friend; being depressed; you or your partner getting pregnant when you do not want this; being abused; other bad troubles.

The third measure, the well-being score, was the average rating (from 1 = very true to 3 = not true), which the young person gave to the following set of statements: I have been doing well at school; there are lots of things I enjoy in my spare time; I have good friends; I am getting on with my family or partner; I have enough money; my health is fine; I am feeling confident; I am pleased with the way my life is going.

Although these measures were conceptually distinct and reflected different view-points they were nevertheless strongly correlated.

On the outcome measures only a minority of the young people who left foster care for independent living were doing well. These were likely to be young mothers who had support from their partner and family or the small group who went on to study at university. But the majority had not achieved stable housing, were only marginal-ly, if at all involved in employment, and were vulnerable to a wide variety of troubles including loneliness, unemployment, depression and lack of money.

Most of these young people needed and indeed received support from a wide variety of people. Informal support was given by members of their birth families, partners and their families, as well as friends and neighbours. Youth, health and social service workers provided more formal support. Foster carers often played a very important role in providing encouragement and back-up support, but this was usually finan-cially or formally unacknowledged.

The study identifies three variables that distinguished those who were doing well from those who were less successful.

First, those young people who were assessed as disturbed at the first contact – three years earlier – had poorer outcomes on all the three measures. And this assessment of disturbance (the Goodman score) was itself correlated with other key variables: performance at school, placement disruption, low involvement in work and a high degree of childlike attachment (attachment disorder).

Second, a strong attachment to at least one adult was associated with good outcomes. Some young people were able to establish and maintain good relationships with a member of their birth family from whom they could get support, or a sustained relationship with their foster family, or have good relationships with their partner and their partner's family. There were examples of formalising attachments with foster carers within the study – foster carers being paid a retainer while a young person was at university and then full board when they returned.

However, the research shows that birth family relationships can also be very problematic for some young people both while living with, and leaving, foster care. They may find it difficult to settle in foster care and commit themselves to their foster carers, being emotionally torn between their birth family and their carers. They are also likely to regress educationally and suffer harm when they return home. Also, some young people leaving foster care are unable to psychologically distance themselves from the traumas they have suffered at the hands of their birth families – they are held back from being able to move on from care and find satisfaction with their lives after care (Sinclair et al, 2003). Skuse and Ward also found that young people who returned home after leaving care often felt let down and experienced as much instability as young people living independently (Skuse and Ward, 2004).

Third, and perhaps paradoxically, involvement in work was associated both with trouble and low well-being and with high ratings of success from foster carers and social workers. As Sinclair and colleagues suggest, 'involvement in work is a criterion of success; it is what parents expect of their children. At the same time the work in which these young people are likely to be involved is marginal. The money earned may raise their rents astronomically. If they fall out of work they may fail to act quickly enough to sort out their benefit position' (Sinclair et al, 2003).

In addition to these three variables, a fourth variable, whether the young person was, in the view of social workers and foster carers, ready and willing to leave foster care, was associated with the first outcome measure, 'doing well'. Although this may be difficult to prove – as it could be a case of being wise after the event – other research has highlighted the poor outcomes for those who leave care early, from a breakdown situation and who are not ready or prepared to leave (Biehal et al, 1995; Stein, 1990; Stein and Carey, 1986).

In the United States, *Assessing the effects of foster care: early results from the Casey national alumni study* reports the findings from case records and interviews with 1,087 adults who were fostered between 1966 and 1998 (Pecora et al, 2004). In comparison to 'ordinary' foster care in the United States, Casey provides long-term family foster care with a range of additional support services including financial aid for participation in a range of leisure activities, educational and training scholarships, independent living training, and individual and group therapy.

In terms of outcomes, many former foster young people achieved educational success. High school graduation rates exceeded graduation rates among the general population and foster care alumni in other US studies – although college completion rates (9 per cent) were much lower than the same age general population group (24 per cent).

A 'success index' was constructed based upon alumni data from at least three of five outcome areas: years of education; household income; physical health; mental health; and relationship satisfaction. The study found that the main variables predicting success in adulthood for the former foster young people were completing high school before leaving care, being in college or on a job training scholarship and support programme; having life skills and independent living training; participating in youth clubs or organisations while in care; not being homeless within one year of leaving care and not requiring alcohol or drug treatment. Being male was a modest predictor.

The study also identifies three 'counter intuitive' predictors. First, 'less positive parenting from the last foster mother'. It is suggested that 'it could be the foster mother's lack of support helped motivate the youth to prepare more vigorously for their emancipation, because vital areas of support were not present and were not likely to continue'(Pecora et al, 2004, p41). Second and third, 'more tutoring' and 'more treatment for drugs and alcohol' were likely to be indicative of greater levels of need and problems.

Additional analyses of high school completion rates show that it is associated with delaying entry into care through primary prevention and family support; placement stability, being in foster care for a longer period of time, reducing placement disruptions; promoting a positive relationship between the young person and the foster parents; providing independent living training; gaining employment experience whilst in care; and minimising criminal behaviour.

Outcome groups

Finally, is it possible to identify outcome groups from the different quantitative and qualitative studies – in regard to how the experience of life in and after leaving care helps or hinders young people? Research studies completed since the 1980s suggest that in broad terms young people leaving care fall into one of three groups: the 'moving on' group, the 'survivors' group, or the 'victims' group (Stein and Carey, 1986; Stein, 1990; Biehal et al, 1995; Dixon and Stein, 2002; Jackson et al, 2003; Sinclair et al, 2003; Pecora et al, 2004).

Moving on

> I feel more of a person now that I'm on my own and I ain't got to go and ask permission from social services for this and that and the other. I feel like myself now, more normal. (Care leaver, in Biehal et al, 1995)

The first group, those 'moving on', are likely to have had stability and continuity in their lives, including a secure attachment relationship; made sense of their family relationships so they could psychologically move on from them; and to have achieved some educational success before leaving care. Their preparation had been gradual, they had left care later and their moving on was likely to have been planned. Being 'more normal' – a post-care normalising identity – through, for example, participating in further or higher education, having a job they liked – but not any job – or being a parent themselves, played a significant part.

Indeed, there is evidence from some young mothers who have been in care of a feeling of maturity and status, thus contributing to achieving an adult identity (Sinclair et al, 2003). The gains included a renewal of family links and improved relationships with their mothers and their partners' families. Hutson (1997) found that young mothers in supported accommodation tended to experience less poverty and reduced social isolation than other care leavers.

The 'moving on' group were also more likely to be young women. Not only were they generally better qualified educationally than young men but they also were able to manage better – being twice as likely to have good practical skills, especially managing money and managing their accommodation by maintaining reasonable relations with landlords, neighbours and friends.

There is also evidence from a study carried out during the 1980s that young people who had successful transitions out of care not only accessed more resources but also had a lot more interactive relationships. They were, for example, able to negotiate decent housing, derive meaningful employment or work, participate in community and leisure activities, and engage in education. This study found that these young people's social networks became richer, more amenable to expansion or contraction at will and their personal states more relaxed, stable and fulfilled. They were less lonely and isolated (Hart, 1984). The same study also found that those whose after-care experience was most successful were those who participated in 'general' or open access activities and opportunities as distinct from 'specialist' care provision, 'which enclose and socially segment care leavers within a whole range of well meaning but misguided provisions' (Hart, 1984, p20).

The 'moving on' group welcomed the challenge of independent living and gaining more control over their lives – often contrasting this with the restrictions imposed while living in care, including the lack of opportunities to make or participate in decisions which affected their lives. They have seen this as improving their confidence and self-esteem. In general, their resilience has been enhanced by their experiences after care and they have been able to make good use of the help they have been offered, often maintaining contact and support from former carers (Schofield, 2001; Sinclair et al, 2003).

Surviving

> I've become more independent, more tough, I know more about the world. (Care leaver, in Stein, 1990)

The second group, the 'survivors', had experienced more instability, movement and disruption while living in care than the 'moving on' group. They were also likely to leave care younger, with few or no qualifications, and often following a breakdown in foster care or a sudden exit from their children's home. They were likely to experience further movement and problems after leaving care, including periods of homelessness, low-paid casual or short-term, unfulfilling work and unemployment. They were also likely to experience problems in their personal and professional relationships through patterns of detachment and dependency.

Many in this group saw themselves as 'more tough', as having done things 'off my own back' and as 'survivors' since leaving care. They believed that the many problems they had faced, and often were still coping with, had made them more grown-up and self-reliant – although their view of themselves as independent was often contradicted by the reality of high degrees of agency dependency for assistance with accommodation, money and personal assistance.

There is research evidence that what made the difference to their lives was the personal and professional support they received after leaving care. Specialist leaving care workers, key workers, as well as mentors – the latter identified in the international review as a resilience-promoting factor (Newman and Blackburn, 2002a and 2002b) – could assist these young people. Assisting young people in finding and maintaining their accommodation is critical to their mental health and well-being (Dixon et al, 2004). Families may also help, but returning to them may prove very problematic for some young people. Overall, some combination of support networks could help them overcome their very poor starting points at the time of leaving care and thus promote their resilience (Biehal et al, 1995; Clayden and Stein, 2002; Dixon and Stein, 2002; Marsh and Peel, 1999).

Being a victim

> I was in a bed-sit on my own, I couldn't handle it, being on my own, being lonely, no family behind me, no friends. I was stopping at home, being bored; I got into financial difficulties and was evicted. (Care leaver, in Stein, 1990)

The third group of care leavers was the most disadvantaged. They had the most damaging pre-care family experiences and, in the main, care was unable to compensate them, to help them overcome their past difficulties. Their lives in care were likely to include many further placement moves, the largest number of moves in the different research studies, and related disruption to their lives, especially in relation to their personal relationships and education. They were also likely to have a cluster of difficulties while in care that often began earlier, including emotional and behavioural difficulties, problems at school and getting into trouble (Dixon et al, 2004). They were the least likely to have a redeeming relationship with a family member or carer. They were likely to leave care younger, following a placement breakdown. At the time of leaving care their life chances were very poor indeed.

After leaving care they were likely to be unemployed, become homeless and have great difficulties in maintaining their accommodation. They were also highly likely to be lonely, isolated and have mental health problems. Aftercare support was unlikely to be able to help them overcome their very poor starting points and they also lacked or alienated personal support. But it was important to these young people that somebody was there for them.

Key messages

- Outcome studies of leaving care services have shown that specialist schemes can successfully assist many young people with their accommodation and life skills, and to a lesser extent with social networks, personal relationships and self-esteem.
- Positive educational and related career outcomes are more closely associated with placement stability, more likely to be achieved in foster care, more associated with gender (young women being far more likely to succeed) and with a supportive environment for study.
- There is also evidence that having a good self-image, and building satisfactory social networks and personal relationships was associated with supportive relationships with family members and former foster carers.
- Research from the United States into preparation programmes highlights the importance of assessment, the need for services to address both 'hard' (practical) and 'soft' (personal) skills, and the importance of targeted services.
- Research evidence shows that young people who go on to higher education in the UK are more likely to have had a stable care experiences, continuity in their schooling, been encouraged by their birth parents – even though they were unable to care for them – and have been greatly assisted by their foster carers in their schooling.
- Young people leaving foster care in England who did well had experienced a strong compensatory attachment with a partner or partner's family, foster carer or family member. Also, they were less likely to be 'disturbed' when first interviewed three years before leaving – and this measure was also correlated with school performance, placement disruption and attachment disorder. Involvement in work, although seen by carers as an indication of success, could be problematic for young people, especially if short-term, unfulfilling and low-paid. Young people being ready, prepared and wanting to move on was also associated with 'doing well'.

- In the United States, young people placed with Casey foster carers who did well as adults, were likely to have completed their high school education, attended college or job training, acquired life skills and independent living training, participated in youth clubs or organisations while in care and were less likely to be homeless within one year of leaving care.
- Drawing on these different studies three outcome groups were proposed: young people 'moving on' – who were able to achieve a post care identity; 'survivors' – who were just coping but whose outcomes were closely linked to the professional and personal support they received; and 'victims' – who were very disadvantaged and would need sustained support.

6 What works in practice?

What can we learn from leaving care research about practice? It is this question that will be explored in this chapter, drawing upon the studies introduced so far, the findings from a survey of best practice carried out during 1999 as well as other project evaluations and practice initiatives (Stein and Wade, 2000). The material introduced, other than where identified as practice examples, will be derived from research findings, but this will include single descriptive project evaluations as well as outcome studies. These different sources of evidence will be discussed in relation to the new responsibilities contained within the Children (Leaving Care) Act 2000.

Providing support: personal advisers and mentors

They're there when you need 'em. (Young person, in Biehal et al, 1995)

One of the main reasons why leaving care schemes were able to achieve successful outcomes was that young people had a leaving care worker who could assist them in meeting their core needs. This meant keeping in touch with them and offering personal and practical support, helping them with accommodation, assisting them with their careers, and helping them access the other services they needed. But it was not just what they did. Many specialist leaving care workers were very committed to young people, and had the skills to engage and involve them. They could work with young people, not just for them (Biehal et al, 1995).

The Children (Leaving Care) Act 2000 recognised this by requiring local authorities to appoint personal advisers to provide advice and support, to play a key role in needs assessment and pathway planning, to co-ordinate services, to be informed about young people and to keep in touch with them. In some authorities the personal adviser role is being carried out by the Connexions service and in others by special-ist leaving care workers. Also, in some authorities partnership arrangements have been developed with voluntary organisations to provide leaving care services, to give young people with a worker some independence from social services. Involving another agency is seen as helping the young person move on, as part of a 'rite de passage'.

Evaluation of different practice initiatives which work well suggests personal support should be based on the following principles (Frost and Stein, 1995; Stein and Wade, 2000). It should be planned and negotiated with young people; be pro-active – not just responding to a crisis; be flexible given the diversity and variety of needs of young people; and be holistic – addressing the practical, financial and emotional needs of young people. A significant challenge to the provision of specialist leaving care support, and one which will be discussed in Chapter 7, is in maintaining continuity in young people's lives, especially positive links with family, carers, friends and their locality. A failure to achieve this can result in sharp divisions between care, leaving care and after care.

The Act also defines 'the responsible local authority' as the one which last 'looked after' a qualifying young person, wherever the young person may be living in England or Wales in order to prevent disputes between local authorities and re-enforce the continuity of care in young people's support arrangements.

Under the Act, it is envisaged that the personal adviser will occupy the central role in assessing needs and planning personal support whatever the organisational arrangements or location. Training will play an important part in the quality of service (Stein et al, 2001). As described in Chapter 3, there are advantages in having a team base which is accessible and young people feel free to drop in to, so that the service is more than just the individual support provided by the personal adviser (Biehal et al, 1995; Wakefield Accomodation Project, 1996; Dixon and Stein, 2002).

Mentoring

> But she was always there you knew, she was always there for me. If I had a problem I could tell her about it and she would help me deal with it. (Mentored young person, in Clayden and Stein, 2002)

Mentoring schemes may also offer support to young people leaving care. They can be seen as occupying a space between formal or professional care and the informal care by families or friends, in assisting care leavers during their journey to adulthood. Rutter's research on resilience, discussed in Chapter 7, has given support to mentoring by highlighting the importance of a caring and consistent adult in the lives of vulnerable young people to help them overcome a range of problems (Rutter, 1987; Rutter et al, 1998). A review of the research literature on mentoring concludes that mentoring programmes cannot stand alone in meeting the needs of young people, particularly at the time of transition from care – they need to be part of a wider system of support (Greim, 1995).

An evaluation of the outcomes of mentoring 39 young care leavers after 6–12 months showed that 60 per cent were still involved in mentoring relationships and most of these young people (81 per cent) had only one mentor. Over a third of the young people had seen their mentor more them 10 times and this was supplemented with contact by telephone, text messaging, e-mail and letter. Just over half of these young people had a personal goal and of these, nearly two-thirds were helped to achieve them. This included improving their practical circumstances (education, employment, housing), improving their living skills (eg, budgeting) and building their confidence and self-esteem. Mentors helped young people achieve their goals by encouraging and listening to them and offering practical help. Most of the young people found their mentor very or fairly helpful to them. This included help with hobbies and interests, communication skills, decision-making, self-confidence and goal-setting (Clayden and Stein, 2002).

Needs assessment and pathway planning

'Has the pathway plan been useful?' 'It has, if you can see the bigger picture, it shows you what you need to work on and what you are ok at.' (Young person, in Hai and Williams, 2004)

Local authorities are given new duties under the Children (Leaving Care) Act 2000 to assess the needs of young people with a view to determining what advice, assistance and support to provide, and to prepare a pathway plan based on the assessment, keeping the plan under regular review. The regulations require the assessment to address health and development, education, employment and training, personal support from family and other relationships, financial needs, practical and other skills necessary for independent living, and young people's needs for care, support and accommodation. In addition to these areas, albeit worded slightly differently, the pathway plans require that contingency planning be undertaken. It is a requirement under the Act for both needs assessments and pathway plans to be recorded, and the young person must be provided with a copy of the pathway plan (Department of Health, 2001a).

Research and evaluations of best practice suggest that a number of elements are associated with smooth and well-planned transitions (Biehal et al, 1995; Stein and Wade, 2000).

To begin with, it helps for planning to take place early on. It should build upon the young person's existing assessment and care plan. Second, the process must involve and empower the young person. The regulations require that the young person's wishes and feelings are taken into account and the guidance identifies the importance of scheduling meetings at convenient times, paying travel expenses and taking account of any disability the young person may have (Department of Health, 2001a). As a practice example, one authority has developed a 'Platform and Roller coaster' pack with young care leavers, a local arts group and two local leaving care teams.

> Platform (this pack) has been designed for you to use with your personal adviser to work out what you need and want. It will be started when you first join the leaving care team and completed within three months, so that the service can provide the right kind of support over the next few years. Platform includes creative workshops, group activities and fun exercises, as well as questions to answer about different life subjects. Your personal adviser will guide this activity, which will help you to get to know each other and to talk about your goals and ambitions as well as any problems that you might have. Your Pathway Plan (Roller coaster) will then be used to plan and review actions that help you to achieve your goals and get to where you want to be. Your personal adviser will speak to other relevant people such as your parents, carers, school and anybody else who you want involved. (Harding, 2001)

Some local authorities have developed skills and expertise in involving young people at a policy level as well as at an individual level – contributing to a more collective view of needs and planning.

One authority has set up a children's panel of councillors and young people in and leaving care to make sure that young people can impact upon decisions that affect their lives. Eleven young people sit on the panel alongside eight councillors and as a sub-committee of the council the panel reports directly to the executive. The structure and process of the meetings have been adapted to make them user-friendly for young people, who set the agenda for each meeting by tabling issues that are of direct concern to them and their peers. Also, the meeting is attended by the head of children's services and service managers who are accountable to the panel for progressing decisions made by the panel and reporting back. Young people are assisted in developing their participation skills by an independent children's rights co-ordinator and members of the 16-plus team. Achievements include a revision to the policy of overnight stays for young people and the development of a video, leaflets and an interactive game to help young people contribute to their reviews (Department of Health/Centrepoint, 2002).

Third, all those with an interest in the support of the young person must be fully involved in the process, provided that this is consistent with the young person's wishes (Biehal et al, 1995; Stein and Wade, 2000). In addition to the young person and their personal adviser, the regulations require that parents, carers, teachers, independent visitors, and general practitioners should normally be involved, as well as anyone else whom the young person or local authority consider relevant (Department of Health, 2001a). Finally, there is also strong evidence that where specialist leaving care schemes exist, they need to be integrated into this process at an early point (Biehal et al, 1995; Stein and Wade, 2000).

Research carried out since the introduction of the Children (Leaving Care) Act has explored the views of young people, social workers and service managers on needs assessment and pathway plans (Hai and Williams, 2004).

Young people were positive about the process, seeing needs assessment and pathway planning as an opportunity to reflect on the past and focus on the future, identifying clear goals and how they will be helped to meet them. They saw the process as working well when they had a good, consistent and stable relationship with their social worker (personal adviser). This was the most important factor in their continued engagement. For those who had a poor relationship it was seen as another paper exercise.

Both social workers and service managers welcomed needs assessment and pathway planning as one of the most beneficial and innovatory parts of the Act. They were seen as very good tools for working with young people by providing formal mechanisms for reviewing, planning and monitoring young people's progress (Hai and Williams, 2004).

Preparation for adult life

The guidance to the Children (Leaving Care) Act identifies three main dimensions to preparation: helping young people to build and maintain relationships with others; enabling young people to develop their self-esteem, including knowledge of their own personal histories and that of their families, cultures and communities; and assisting young people to acquire practical and financial skills and knowledge (Department of Health, 2001a).

Evaluations of good practice in regard to preparation point to the importance of assessment to identify young people's needs and how they will be met (part of the needs assessment process under the Act); providing ongoing support and opportunities for participation, involving discussion, negotiation and risk-taking; and the gradual learning of skills, in the context of a stable placement (Clayden and Stein, 1996; Lynes and Goddard, 1995). However, achieving such stability for young people in care, especially those living in children's homes, is a major challenge (Sinclair and Gibbs, 1998; Whitaker et al, 1998; Berridge and Brodie, 1998).

Research into the quality of care in children's homes has indicated that homes are likely to achieve positive outcomes if they are small; the head of home feels that its roles are clear, mutually compatible, and not disturbed by frequent reorganisation and that they are given adequate autonomy to get on with the job; and the staff are agreed about how the home should be run and are not at odds with each other (Sinclair and Gibbs, 1998). The same research also stressed the importance of tackling bullying and unwanted sexual advances – both factors that contributed to the misery of residents. Also, support and encouragement, the teaching of practical skills, moving on when ready, and ongoing support after care, were all seen as important by young people and their social workers in retrospect (Sinclair and Gibbs, 1998). Smit, in her research into preparation for leaving residential care in Holland, found that a more positive attitude towards discharge and the more perceived support available, the more likely a successful outcome (Smit, 1995)

Also, preparation should attach equal importance to practical, emotional and interpersonal skills and be responsive to ethnic diversity and any disability the young person may have (Rabiee et al, 2001). Specialist leaving care schemes can assist carers with the development of skills training programmes, and by offering intensive compensatory help at the aftercare stage (Biehal et al, 1995; Clayden and Stein, 1996).

Practice examples include: a peer education preparation programme employing care leavers on a sessional basis to deliver training to young people in care, informing them about the realities of independent living; a resource pack to help carers support black and minority ethnic young people to explore their cultural issues; training for foster carers and residential workers so that they have clear expectations of what preparation work they will be expected to undertake with young people; and the direct involvement of young people in the preparation of materials including a care leaver's diary, a cookbook and an interactive CD-ROM and video (Department of Health/Centrepoint, 2002).

Informal support: family links

Until recently, research into family links had generally identified the advantages to care leavers. For example, it has been suggested that wherever it proves possible, young people's interests will be served best by efforts to maintain or create links with their families while they are looked after (Milham et al, 1986). Even if relationships with parents have broken down, other members of a young person's extended family may be able to offer some support (Marsh and Peel, 1999; Dixon and Stein, 2002). There is also evidence that contact with family can contribute to a positive self-image (Biehal et al, 1995). Also, at a later point, those lacking family support may have greater difficulty creating new relationships (Biehal et al, 1995) and, as detailed earlier, black and minority ethnic young people isolated from family and community may experience identity problems (Ince, 1998).

However, as discussed in Chapter 5, Sinclair and colleagues' study of foster care describes how some young people leaving foster care are psychologically held back by their birth families from being able to move on from care and find satisfaction in their lives after care, and Biehal and Wade's analysis of family realtionships also shows the problematic nature of family relationships for some young people after care (Sinclair et al, 2003; Biehal and Wade, 1996).

Best practice will be assisted by a realistic assessment of young people's sources of family, carer and informal support at the planning stage. This may include arrangements for young people to live close to supports, a continuing role for carers to support young people and the option for young people to remain with carers on a supported lodging basis (Fry, 1992; Wade, 1997; Dixon and Stein, 2002). There is also evidence that specialist leaving care schemes can play an important role in helping young people form new networks and relationships (Biehal et al, 1995).

As a practice example, family group conferences – traditionally associated with child protection – have been used to include families in the decision-making process for young people leaving care. In one area, an independent co-ordinator arranges a meeting between a young person, their social worker and agreed relatives, friends and professionals, in order to discuss the young person's needs and plan the role to be played by family members and other people able to offer support after care (Department of Health/Centrepoint, 2002).

Health and development

The neglect of both disability and the health needs of young people leaving care in the research literature has been discussed in Chapter 3 – and thus the evidence base for good practice is limited (Broad, 2003; Rabiee et al, 2001; Stein and Wade, 2000).

The available evidence points to the need for these areas to be given far more priority (Berridge and Brodie, 1998; Farmer and Pollock, 1997; Saunders and Broad, 1997; Rabiee et al, 2001). The best practice survey suggests that health care may be assisted by a thorough health assessment and the maintenance of detailed health records while young people are looked after. Pathway plans should build upon what has gone before to promote a healthy lifestyle. This may include: appropriate use of primary care services, access to specialist mental health and therapeutic services where necessary and the promotion of leisure services (Department of Health, 1997; Stein and Wade, 2000). There is evidence from research in Scotland that foster carers would welcome more guidance, support and information on mental health issues, sexual health, sexuality and relationships, to enable them to develop confidence, knowledge and skills in supporting young people. In the same study, foster carers described their main problems as accessing psychological services; not having sufficient information before a placement; and their efforts to introduce healthy lifestyles being undermined by birth families and young people's peers (Scottish Health Feedback, 2003).

As regards young disabled people leaving care, the implication of Priestley and colleagues' (2003) and Hai and Williams's (2004) research is that a lot remains to be done at both a strategic and operational level to link the services and expertise within disabilities teams, leaving care projects and adult services. Also, Rabiee and colleagues (2001) argue for developments in monitoring, planning, supporting transitions, promoting involvement and training, to improve policy and practice for young disabled people leaving care.

Although as yet not evaluated, a number of recent initiatives have been identified in local authorities management action plans under the Quality Protects initiative (Wade, 2003) and in the Department of Health/Centrepoint publication *Care leaving strategies: a good practice handbook* (2002). These include:

service level agreements with primary care teams and child and adolescent mental health services (CAMHS)

- multi-disciplinary teams or secondments (including CAMHS staff)
- partnerships with Health Promotion to audit needs, provide training and information
- peer education initiatives to offer advice on healthy living to looked-after young people
- initiatives around drugs, sexual health, teenage pregnancy and supporting young families
- projects to promote positive mental health through a confidential listening service and access to advocacy, information and advice
- providing care leavers with a discount leisure pass
- peer support programme for lesbian, gay and bisexual young people.

Post-16 careers: education, employment and training

Improving the education, employment and training outcomes for care leavers is recognised within the Act by the requirement to provide financial assistance and social support to be available for education, training or work up to the age of 21 (or 24 if continuing in education), as well as in the Quality Protects targets. It is also to be an important aspect of needs assessment and pathway planning.

Enhancing the career chances of care leavers needs to build upon the educational progress while young people are looked after. This is clearly recognised in the Social Exclusion Unit's report, *A better education for children in care* (SEU, 2003). The need for five key changes is spelt out: greater stability; less time out of school; help with schoolwork; more help from home to support schoolwork; and improved health and well-being. There is evidence that placement stability, positive encouragement, pro-active placement, school and education service links, as well as compensatory assistance, can be helpful to young people (Biehal et al, 1995; Menmuir, 1994; Walker, 1994; McParlin, 1996; SEU, 2003). Conversely, teachers' negative attitudes, low expectations, bullying and giving little priority to education, may all inhibit young people's educational progress (Jackson, 1994; Parker et al, 1991). However, as suggested in Chapter 3, the problems are even more challenging – as they are also associated with what happens to young people before they enter care, including for some young people their very damaging intra-family relations.

There is also evidence from evaluated practice that young people can be assisted by: assessing their skills and abilities, including any achievements and potential; providing ongoing support to maintain motivation and to assist those wishing to return to learning, and remain in training or employment (Wade, 2003).

In England, the Coram Education Service provides young people leaving care with a bridge to further education, training and employment. It works with young people with major educational deficits through individual and group basic skills teaching as well as teaching in four core subjects: IT, English, mathematics and art. Accreditation is available in all of these subjects and support is provided through individual advice and a range of educational facilities. Each young person is allocated a personal tutor with direct responsibility for their educational development.

An evaluation of the service, covering the academic years 1999–2002, demonstrated its success in getting young people, the majority of whom were unemployed (81 per cent) when starting, back into education. Of those unemployed at the outset, 21 per cent were attending college full time, 6 per cent part time and 16 per cent were continuing to use the service. Only 15 per cent were still unemployed. For 14 of the 20 young people who were in education at referral, the majority of these were continuing in education. The service was equally successful in engaging black and minority ethnic young people, young men and young women. This type of service enables young people who have missed out educationally to get back on the education ladder – a bridge to learning (Clayden, 2003).

The post-16 section of the Social Exclusion Unit's 2003 report acknowledges the long shadow cast by poor educational attainment in terms of the low take-up of further and higher education – although as Broad's 2002–2003 survey shows, the percentage of young people participating in further education has increased since the introduction of the Children (Leaving Care) Act in October 2001 (Broad, 2003). Also the report stresses the need care leavers have for additional support to re-engage in learning and cope with the demands of student life while at the same time adjusting to living independently (Post-16 SEU, 2003).

It is estimated that less than 1 per cent of care leavers go on to study in higher education compared to about 40 per cent of their peers (Jackson et al, 2003). The University of Southampton runs a summer school for young people from inner city areas and care leavers to give them a sample of life at university. During the week the care leavers stay in university halls of residence and take part in an academic programme of their choice including science, engineering, social sciences, law and humanities. The programme, which in part is run by existing students, includes communication skills, teamwork and self-esteem as well as a lively programme of social activities (Department of Health/Centrepoint, 2002).

A London borough provides a range of services to increase university uptake among young people in care. This includes a specialist teacher in post-16 education to offer advice on courses, interview preparation and help with university application forms. The scheme also provides life skills training and financial support of up to £5,000 annually to cover subsistence and accommodation costs. Does it make a difference? Well, it seems to. Nine per cent of its care leavers are at university compared with a national average of 1 per cent cited above (Post-16 SEU, 2003).

Also, inter-agency links can provide access to career opportunities and to plan service developments – including links with Connexions, training agencies, further and higher education colleges, employers, benefits agencies and youth services (Department of Health, 1997; Smith, 1994; Post-16 SEU, 2003; Wade, 2003). A number of local authorities have been successful in developing work experience placements for care leavers through collaborative working and the Who Cares? Trust Employability Programme (Department of Health/Centrepoint, 2002).

In two county council areas, covering one Connexions area, a partnership agreement has been introduced. The perceived benefits of this joint approach include: joint ownership of targets aimed at helping care leavers succeed in their transition to working life and adulthood; more awareness of the services available and how they may be accessed; better working relationships and a more seamless service (Post-16 SEU, 2003).

Finance

Maximising young people's educational and career opportunities is the best way to protect young people against poverty and subsequent dependency on benefits – although, as already detailed in Chapter 5, the research evidence reveals high levels of unemployment and low levels of attainment and participation in education and training among care leavers.

Under the Children (Leaving Care) Act 2000, the local authority has become the sole agency responsible for providing financial assistance to qualifying 16- and 17-

year-old young care leavers (excluding disabled young people and lone parents). Young people welcome receiving their payments directly into a bank account as this is non-stigmatising and helps them to understand personal finance as well as to handle money. There is evidence that the transfer of financial assistance to local authorities has contributed to the increased participation of young people in further education (Broad, 2003).

Personal advisers will still have a key role in accessing financial assistance for care leavers once they are 18 years old. Research studies have shown the importance of providing clear, accessible information to all parties as well as developing formal links and protocols with relevant agencies (Biehal et al, 1995; Broad, 1998; First Key, 1996; Department of Health, 1997).

Practice examples include comprehensive and accessible local guides to inform young people of the help and support they can expect to receive, including their legal status under the Children (Leaving Care) Act 2000; and cross-authority protocols so that young people who move from the 'responsible authority' are able to receive financial support outside of their area (Department of Health/Centrepoint, 2002).

Accommodation

Young people leaving care are a diverse group whose accommodation needs will vary according to gender, ethnicity and sexuality. Disability and physical and mental health should be considered in planning accommodation. The Children (Leaving Care) Act requires local authorities to provide 'suitable' accommodation, and the Homelessness Act 2002 extends the priority needs groups to include former care leavers who are homeless between the ages of 18 and 21.

There is substantial evidence that specialist leaving care services have been successful in developing a range of accommodation for young people leaving care, including supported carer schemes, re-designating foster placements as supported lodgings, provision offering accommodation plus support (such as 'trainer' flats, supported hostels and floating support schemes), foyers and independent tenancies (Stein, 1990; Stone, 1990; Fry, 1992; Anderson and Quilgars, 1995; Wade, 1997; Broad, 1998; Biehal and Wade, 1999; Dixon and Stein, 2002). However, there is also evidence of gaps in provision. Foyers, because of their low levels of staffing, may find it difficult to respond to the needs of very vulnerable care leavers or homeless young people with multiple problems (Hutson and Liddiard, 1994; Hutson, 1995). Centrepoint's work in seven London boroughs uncovered gaps in the provision of high-level support for very vulnerable young people as well as short-break and emergency accommodation (Department of Health/Centrepoint, 2002).

In order to meet their statutory responsibilities many housing and social service departments have developed joint protocols and multi-agency accommodation strategies. This has included working together on needs assessment and in some areas joint training between housing and social services.

In one London borough integrated service provision has been achieved by seconding the housing commissioning manager to work within the leaving care team in a new role as the Corporate Parent (Housing Needs). This officer has the specific remit of developing housing options for young people leaving care and commissioning new contracts for interim accommodation with the private and public sector. The officer is also responsible for processing all housing applications for care leavers to ensure that offers of housing are appropriate to the needs of individual young people. The post has helped to develop good partnership arrangements between housing and social services and the introduction of new procedures and monitoring systems (Department of Health/Centrepoint, 2002).

The needs assessment and pathway planning process envisages housing and social services carrying out joint assessments. Evaluations of practice suggest that when planning to meet the needs of individual young people, positive outcomes will be assisted by: avoiding moving young people who are settled – letting young people remain with foster carers when settled through re-designating placements as supported lodgings is simple and effective; involving young people in planning and decision-making; assessing accommodation needs; preparing young people; offering a choice in the type and location of accommodation, taking into account any physical, sensory or learning impairment they may have; having a contingency plan; setting up a package of support to go with the accommodation; and having a clear financial plan (Hutson, 1995; Stein and Wade, 2000; Wade, 2003).

Contingency plans

The Children (Leaving Care) Act requires, 'contingency plans for action to be taken by the responsible authority should the pathway plan for any reason cease to be effective'.

As detailed in Chapter 3, young people leaving care often have compressed and accelerated transitions to adulthood. It is not surprising that many experience difficulties and crises after leaving care and, as research into leaving care services in London found, young people want access to 24-hour support (Hai and Williams, 2004). Research evidence also indicates that few have the opportunity to return to care or sheltered provision, and that young people may have difficulty in reconciling themselves to such a return (Biehal et al, 1995; Department of Health, 1997). Also, as indicated above, there are specific gaps in the provision of short-break care.

Evidence of successful contingency arrangements includes returning to successful foster care arrangements or emergency lodgings. An example of specifically designated housing provision is an eight-bedded housing scheme in which four of the rooms are used for ongoing accommodation and the remaining four are reserved for emergency or short-break use, and only paid for when occupied. This allows the commissioning authority to access approved and safe emergency bed spaces (Department of Health/Centrepoint, 2002). Some local authorities have also set up 24-hour telephone helplines for care leavers – someone there for them to talk to when in a crisis (Department of Health/Centrepoint, 2002).

Specialist leaving care schemes have been particularly effective in assisting young people through specialist worker support and access to a range of accommodation options. Their responsive approach also encourages young people to seek help when they are in difficulty, lonely or desperate (Biehal et al, 1995; Broad, 1998).

Key messages

This review of evaluated practice draws upon a wide range of evidence – from descriptions of single projects to larger outcome studies. Some of the 'evidence' is what young people and practitioners see or think is working for them. Other evidence is derived from qualitative studies, surveys and outcome research. These different sources provide pointers to guide good practice post the Children (Leaving Care) Act 2000:

- the key role of personal advisers in needs assessment, pathway planning and providing personal support;
- the positive contribution of mentoring schemes;
- involving and empowering young people both at an individual and policy level;

- adopting a holistic approach in preparing young people, by attaching equal importance to practical, emotional and interpersonal needs;
- developing informal as well as formal support networks based on careful assessments;
- giving more priority to young people's health and developmental needs;
- furthering strategic and operational integration between leaving care services, disabilities teams and adult services;
- sharing best practice in post-16 careers and accommodation projects and initiatives;
- developing contingency arrangements;
- working with different agencies;
- responding to the diverse needs of young people.

7 What works in theory?

How does the research introduced in this text connect with different theoretical perspectives? Undoubtedly, a weakness of much of the work reviewed is a failure to make explicit its theoretical underpinning and explore, empirically, theoretical notions. There are few theoretical moments. It has been argued in relation to the study of adolescence generally that a wide range of empirical research provides little support for 'classical' psychoanalytical or sociological theories, which misrepresent 'normal' adolescence as a time of great psychological disturbance or deviant behaviour (Coleman and Hendry, 1999). As regards young people leaving care, contributions in the area of attachment theory, focal theory, life course analysis and resilience, are all potentially fruitful in relation to the empirical research discussed thus far.

Attachment theory

Bowlby's seminal theoretical work on attachment and loss and its further development by other researchers has documented the impact of actual or threatened separation on young children and patterns of behaviour produced by unsatisfactory interaction with parents, as well as separations per se (Bowlby, 1973; 1982a; Ainsworth and Eichberg, 1991). Children's attachment patterns have been classified into four different types: secure; insecure/avoidant; insecure/ambivalent; and disorganised/unresolved (Crittenden, 1992). Research has also explored how disturbances in attachment are reflected in the way a child sees the world and processes information and how these processes may lead to enduring styles of relationships in childhood, adolescence and adulthood (Crittenden, 1992; Downes, 1992; Bretherton, 1991).

More specifically, Downes draws on attachment theory to offer a framework for understanding adolescents' reactions to the experience of being fostered. Her work is based on an intensive study of the interaction between fostered adolescents and foster family members in 23 time-limited placements over a two-and-a-half-year period.

Arising out of the detailed analysis of the interaction between adolescents and foster carers, in the light of attachment theory, Downes deduces five principles.

- First, as a result of their previous experience, many adolescents who are looked after by the local authority have considerable difficulties in using other people's help; either they are only able to fend for themselves or they repeatedly subvert their own efforts to cope and to make satisfying relationships. Their difficulties in making alliances with helpful adults and peers are likely to put them at a disadvantage when they are trying to make their way in the world as young adults. The remedy therefore has to be more complicated than merely offering adolescents opportunities to learn practical 'survival skills' before they leave care, although these are necessary too (see also Stein and Carey, 1986).
- Second, in an optimum 'secure attachment' position, adolescents and adults are able to feel comfortable in a wide range of interactions within a significant relationship, they are able to enjoy intimacy and also to operate independently at some distance from their family or friends, and they are able to move easily between these positions. In contrast, many adolescents looked after by the local authority lack this flexibility. They may either cling anxiously or keep the people who are important to them at arm's length; they may have difficulties in trusting other people or committing themselves to close relationships with adults or peers.
- Third, these inflexible patterns of behaviour have a tendency to be self-perpetuating, as the adolescents concerned are likely to be active partners in keeping things the same. Change may come about simply through experiencing a different quality of relationship with foster carers, but it is more likely to involve adolescents reflecting on what has happened to them in earlier relationships and exploring the perceptions and feelings that close relationships engender in them.
- Fourth, events involving interaction between adolescents and foster carers on the boundary between the family and the world outside the family may be regarded as potential junction points where change in an adolescent's developmental pathway may occur for better or worse.
- Fifth, while adolescents may begin to trust their foster carers and to gain confidence in negotiating the transition to adult life during the placement, once the placement ends they may not be able to sustain the confidence that reliable adults will be available to help them when needed. This has important implications for aftercare, and in particular for the part that foster carers might play in this.

From these five principles Downes argues that adolescents need to be able to experience their foster carers as a secure base, to provide them with opportunities and active encouragement to explore and become confident in the adult world. It is also suggested that foster carers need to support adolescents' efforts to reappraise their relationships with parents and other significant attachment figures.

> The foster family also needs to be in a position to where they are able to continue to welcome adolescents and young adults back and to support them after the placement ends. This may continue until they have consolidated the changes in their internal model of self in relation to attachment figures so that they eventually have a secure base within themselves. (Downes, 1992, p122)

Attachment theory offers a framework for making sense of the experiences of many young people leaving care (Howe, 1995; Schofield, 2001). For some young people their journey through care has compensated them for their earlier problems. It has provided them with stability and a secure attachment to at least one of their carers. And from this secure base they have been provided with the opportunities and active encouragement to explore and become confident in the adult world. Care has provided them with turning points – by their removal from a damaging family background – and an opportunity to develop their potential in their 'new' families, communities and at school (Rutter et al, 1998; Newman and Blackburn, 2002a).

However, for too many young people, their experiences of care, far from helping them overcome the damaging emotional legacy of family problems, have rendered them unable to form the very relationships they need so much. A consistent finding of studies of care leavers since the 1980s has been the 30 to 40 per cent of young people who experience four plus moves and, within this group, the 6 to 10 per cent who have a very large number of moves – as many as ten or more (see Chapter 3).

The consequence of movement and disruption for many of these young people is to leave them emotionally polarised between dependence and independence, and denied, through their experiences of family and care, the emotional flexibility to find satisfaction in a range of different relationships. As Downes has suggested, many of these young people have great difficulties in using other people's help – either they are only able to fend for themselves or they repeatedly subvert their own efforts to cope and to make satisfying relationships. Their difficulties in making alliances with helpful adults and peers are likely to put them at a disadvantage when they are trying to make their way in the world as young adults (Downes, 1992). But it is not always so. For some young people, the barriers themselves are a way of coping, perhaps more so for the 'independent' than for highly dependent young people.

For some black and minority ethnic young people who experience movement and disruption while living in care there is often the additional burden of isolation from the black community. Unaccompanied young asylum-seekers whose attachments to family, culture, community and country have often been severed very suddenly and who face uncertainty while their immigration status is being processed, can only suffer further in poor-quality temporary accommodation (Kidane, 2002).

The main implication of attachment theory is the need to provide young people with stable placements that can help them overcome their earlier problems and provide them with a strong emotional platform for their journey to adulthood. The relation-ship between providing stability and secure attachment is under-researched. However, it seems likely that the link between stability and improved life chances for care leavers is associated with some care leavers having experienced compensatory secure attachments, especially through long-term fostering. For others, the stability, although not necessarily resulting in secure attachment, has provided them with security and continuity in their lives (Jackson and Thomas, 2001).

Focal theory and transitions

Focal theory or the 'focal model of adolescence' was developed by Coleman partly as an attempt to resolve the contradictions between 'classical' psychoanalytical and soci-ological accounts of adolescence, highlighting its problematic nature and the large number of empirical research studies indicating that for the majority of young people, although major adaptation has to occur, it is a period of relative stability (Coleman, 1974; 1978; 1979; 1980).

The focal model grew out of a study of normal adolescent development which tested large samples of young men and young women at the ages of 11, 13, 15 and 17, and elicited from them attitudes and opinions about a wide range of relationships. Data was gathered on self-image, being alone, sexual relationships, parental relationships, friendships, and large group situations. The material was analysed in terms of the constructive and negative elements present in these relationship situations, and in terms of the common themes expressed by the young people involved in the study. The findings showed that attitudes to all relationships changed as a function of age, but more importantly the results also indicated that concerns about different issues reached a peak at different stages in the adolescent process. For example, conflict with parents peaked at 17, fears of rejection from peer group peaked at 14, and anxiety over sexual relationships peaked at 11 years of age. It was this finding which led to the formation of a 'focal' theory. The model suggests that at different ages particular sorts of relationship patterns come into focus, in the sense of being the most prominent, but that no pattern is specific to one age only. Thus the patterns overlap, different issues come into focus at different times, but simply because an issue is not the most prominent feature of an age does not mean that it may not be critical for some individuals.

Coleman agues that focal theory differs from developmental stage theory in three respects: firstly, the resolution of one issue is not seen as the sine qua non for tackling the next; secondly, the model does not assume the existence of fixed boundaries between stages and, therefore, issues are not necessarily linked to a particular age or developmental level; and thirdly, there is nothing immutable about the sequence involved – although recognising that in our culture individuals are likely to face different issues in early and late adolescence.

Coleman poses the question:

> If adolescents have to adjust to so much potentially stressful change, and at the same time pass through this stage of life with relative stability, as the empirical view indicates, how do they do it? The answer, which is suggested by the 'focal' model, is that they cope by dealing with one issue at a time. They spread the process of adaptation over a span of years, attempting to resolve first one issue, and then the next. Different problems, different relationship issues come into focus and are tackled at different stages, so the stresses resulting from the need to adapt to new modes of behaviour are rarely concentrated all at one time. (Coleman and Hendry, 1999, p207)

The theory has been tested empirically and received support through large research studies carried out in Scotland, the United States and New Zealand (Hendry et al, 1985; Kroger, 1985). In addition, Simmonds and Blythe tested the proposition, contained within the focal model, that those who adjust less well during adolescence are likely to be those who have to face more than one interpersonal issue at a time (Simmonds and Blythe, 1987). The authors documented the life changes occurring for the young people in their study, and related the number of changes to outcome measures such as self-esteem and academic performance. They concluded that among boys and girls, those who experienced a greater number of life changes were at greater risk in terms of the outcome variables.

As regards care leavers, the main message from the studies discussed in Chapter 3 was that in comparison to their peers in the general population, most young people leaving care have to cope with the challenges and responsibilities of major changes in their lives – in leaving foster care or residential care and setting up home; in leaving school and entering the world of work, or more likely, being unemployed and surviving on benefits; and being parents – at a far younger age. In short, many have compressed and accelerated transitions to adulthood that deny the psychological opportunity and space to focus – to deal with issues over time.

However, there are two related dimensions of transition that impact upon young people leaving care and which also need to be considered.

First, as the Joseph Rowntree Foundation's Young People in Transition research programme shows, during the last 20 years patterns of transition into adulthood have been changing fast: the major decline in the youth labour market based on manufacturing and apprenticeship training; the extension of youth training, further and higher education; and the reduction in entitlements to universal welfare benefits for young people. These changes have resulted in young people being more dependent on their families for emotional, financial and practical support, often into their early 20s (Joseph Rowntree Foundation, 2002). In today's 'risk' society, parents, grandparents and other relatives are increasingly occupying a central role at different life stages. Yet the very people who are the most likely to lack the range and depth of help given by families, are expected to cope at a far younger age than young people living with their families.

Second, the process of social transition has traditionally included three distinct, but related, stages: leaving or disengagement; transition itself; and integration into a new or different social state. However, due to the changes outlined above – especially in relation to education, employment and housing, for many young people the overall process is becoming more extended, connected and permeable. For example, further and higher education take place over a longer period of time, young people return home after higher education, and there is growth in temporary and short-term employment markets.

The second stage, transition itself, is critical to this changing process, preparing young people for the 'risk' society. What anthropologists call a 'liminal state' or opportunity to 'space out' provides a time for freedom, exploration, reflection, risk-taking and identity search. For a majority of young people today this is gained through the experience of further and higher education. Yet, as discussed above, many care leavers, as a consequence of their pre-care and care experiences, are unable to take advantage of educational opportunities. Instead, there is the expectation of instant adulthood on leaving care, a conflating of the three distinct stages of social transition into the final stage, to be achieved by the preparatory rigours of domestic combat courses when young people reach 15 years of age.

The implications of focal theory and greater awareness of transitions point to the need for more recognition of the nature and timing of young people's transitions from care. This will include giving young people the emotional and practical support they will need into their early 20s, providing them with the psychological space to cope with changes over time, as well as recognising the different stages of transitions, including the significance of the middle stage, transition and the implications of the increased uncertainties, risks and more fluid nature of social transitions.

Life course theory

Life course theory sees young people's lives as an integrated whole as distinct from a series of separate cycles or developmental stages. It is the inter-connected aspects of the individual life course that are critical: social and historical context – lives in time and space; human agency – the negotiation of personal transitions; social roles and sequential events. It is the interaction between the personal biography and agency of young people and the wider social and economic contexts that may restrict or provide opportunities, which is central to a life course approach (Jones and Wallace, 1992). It therefore challenges a predetermined sequential order and allows for flexibility and variation in the timing and sequencing of events in young people's lives.

Baldwin (1998) and Horrocks (2002) use a life course theory to explore the transitions of young people leaving care. Baldwin carried out three in-depth interviews over a period of 12 months with 16 young people who had grown up in care and 6 young people from similar social backgrounds, who had grown up in their biological families. Horrocks maintained 'informal interview contact' with 14 young people who had left care every two months over a 12–18-month period – carrying out 6–9 interviews. Both studies were ethnographic in orientation, seeing young people as 'active, thinking agents who are capable of making choices and creating their own destinations within given constraints' (Baldwin, p27) and capturing the 'contextual and sequential appreciation' (Horrocks, p328) of young people's lives.

What are the implications of research using life course theory? Both studies highlighted the diversity of young people's biographical experiences and the challenge their experiences pose to standardised or official outcome measures. This includes the failure of such measures to recognise the very different starting points of young people given the diversity of their family backgrounds, needs and care experiences. Their research also questions the separation of outcome measures – 'where measurable outcomes are so clearly inter-connected with an individual's past transitions, current circumstances and personal factors' (Horrocks, 2002, p331). Finally, their findings challenge normative assumptions held by social services about moving on and achieving independence at 18.

Horrocks concludes:

> Does it seem appropriate to suggest that those young people who have probably had to traverse the most arduous developmental process should then 'move on' to have their outcomes measured against some normative ideal with very little accommodation of difference. This observation does not imply that care leavers should be prescribed lower expectations. Rather, it subscribes to the view that the sequential and interactive process of young people's lives should be more comprehensively taken into account when evaluating outcomes. (2002, p335)

A life course approach can be applied to understanding the education and career trajectories of care leavers by exploring their pre-care, care and post-care careers (Stein, 1994).

First, the disadvantaged social class position of families from which many young people enter care and the associated cultural barriers will have a major influence upon their low educational achievement, especially for those young people who enter care during their school years. In addition, white boys from poor backgrounds and black African-Caribbean boys fare worse than girls and boys from higher socio-economic groups. In terms of pre-care careers, young people possess class, gender and ethnic identities, which will influence their educational opportunities.

Second, in addition to these structural identities and cultural influences, most of these young people will have experienced damaging intra-family relations that may have included neglect and poor parenting, or physical, emotional or sexual abuse, experiences that are likely to impact upon their emotional and intellectual development.

Third, against this background, the purpose of care should be to compensate these young people. The foundation stone is stability. However, research completed during the last 20 years has highlighted the high levels of instability and placement disruption, as detailed above in the discussion of attachment theory. Research completed for the Social Exclusion Unit's report found that 14 per cent of young people had three or more placements during the year 2001–2002 and over a third of young people had changed school at least twice as a result of a change in care placement (SEU, 2003). In addition to movement and disruption their difficulties may be compounded by labelling, low carer expectations and practical learning difficulties.

Fourth, looked-after young people are more likely not to be in school than other young people. They are 10 times more likely to be permanently excluded than their peers and there is also evidence of fixed-term unofficial exclusions and poor attendance (SEU, 2003). Also, there may be a failure to compensate young people who have missed out on their schooling, or who have special educational needs (27 per cent have a statement compared to 3 per cent of all children in care, or who have emotional, mental health or physical health problems).

Fifth, many of these young people will experience accelerated and compressed transitions to adulthood.

Finally, the cumulative impact of their pre-care and care careers including their transitions from care, is that many are more likely to be unemployed, be dependent on benefits, and be far less likely to enter higher education than young people in the general population.

Although this example applies a life course approach specifically to young people's education and careers, it could be argued that it is the inter-relationship between their damaging pre-care experiences and what happens to them while in care that contributes to a cluster of poor life chances after care. An exploration of the life course may begin to explain the long-standing nature of many of the problems detailed in Chapter 3 and why there are no simple fixes.

Resilience

Resilience can be defined as the quality that enables some young people to find fulfilment in their lives despite their disadvantaged backgrounds, the problems or adversity they may have undergone or the pressures they may experience. Resilience is about overcoming the odds, coping and recovery. But it is only relative to different risk experiences – relative resistance as distinct from invulnerability – and is likely to develop over time (Rutter, 1999; Schofield, 2001). Also, as has been recognised by a review of the literature on self-esteem, single issue movements, although popular, usually oversimplify complex associations (Elmer, 2001). Resilience may well be just a rose by another name – child development? attachment? (Luthar et al, 2000)

Why some young people cope better than others is complex and there may well be innate and linked personal attributes we do not understand. In the UK the resilience of young people from very disadvantaged family backgrounds has been found to be associated with: a redeeming and warm relationship with at least one person in the family – or secure attachment to at least one unconditionally supportive parent or parent substitute; positive school experiences; feeling able to plan and be in control; being given the chance of a 'turning point', such as a new opportunity or break from a high-risk area; higher childhood IQ scores and lower rates of temperamental risk; and having positive peer influences (Rutter et al, 1998).

A recent research review of the international literature on resilience factors in relation to the key transitions made by children and young people during their lifecycle has added to this picture. As well as the first three factors identified above, the authors conclude that children and young people who are best equipped to overcome adversities will have: strong social support networks; a committed mentor or person from outside the family; a range of extra-curricular activities that promote the learning of competencies and emotional maturity; the capacity to re-frame adversities so that the beneficial as well as the damaging effects are recognised; the ability – or opportunity – to make a difference, for example, by helping others through volunteering, or undertaking part-time work; and exposure to challenging situations which provide opportunities to develop both problem-solving abilities and emotional coping skills (Newman and Blackburn, 2002a and 2002b).

But what of young people from care backgrounds? Although there have been some descriptive accounts and very useful practice guides (Gilligan, 2001) and an important study applying the concept of resilience to 40 adults who grew up in foster care

(Schofield, 2001), there has been little exploration of research focusing solely upon the resilience of young people who have been in care and the implications of these findings for promoting the resilience of care leavers (Stein, forthcoming).

What are the links between the research findings discussed in this publication and the resilience-promoting factors identified above?

First, as detailed in Chapter 5, young people who experience stable placements providing good quality care are more likely to have positive outcomes than those who have experienced further movement and disruption during their time in care. Stability has the potential to promote resilience in two respects. Firstly, it provides the young person with a warm and redeeming relationship with a carer – or as detailed above, in the account of attachment theory, a compensatory secure attachment which may in itself reduce the likelihood of placement breakdown (Rutter et al, 1998). Secondly, and not necessarily dependent on the first, stability may provide continuity of care in young people's lives, which may give them security and contribute to positive educational and career outcomes (Jackson, 2002; Jackson et al, 2003). In promoting resilience, providing stability and continuity may be as important as secure attachment, depending on the age of the young person on entry to care and their history, including the quality of their family relationships and links. Indeed, as recent research on adoptions has shown, not all adopted children and young people are able to form secure attachments – but they can benefit from stability and continuity in their lives (Department of Health, 1999).

Second, helping young people develop a positive sense of identity, including their self-knowledge, their self-esteem and self-efficacy, may also promote their resilience. And although not explicitly recognised as a variable in the research literature on resilience, identity could be seen as connected to, as well as a component of, key associations: feeling able to plan and be in control; the capacity to re-frame adversities so that the beneficial as well as the damaging effects are recognised; personality – or lower rates of temperamental risk (Rutter et al, 1998; Newman and Blackburn, 2002a).

Indeed, identity formation is an ongoing challenge for all young people, as society has become more complex in terms of industrial change, more consumerist in its ideals and less certain in class, gender, geographical and ethnic identities. In what has been described as today's 'risk society', identity formation is a dynamic and reflexive process, less given and pre-determined – but it is a society in which the family plays a central and increasingly extended role (Beck, 1992; Giddens, 1991).

Helping care leavers develop a positive identity will be linked to: firstly, the quality of care and attachments experienced by looked-after young people – a significant resilience-promoting factor discussed above; secondly, to their knowledge and understanding of their background and personal history; thirdly, to their experience of how other people perceive and respond to them; and finally, how they see themselves and the opportunities they have to influence and shape their own biography.

Third, having a positive experience of school, including achieving educational success is associated with resilience among young people from disadvantaged family backgrounds and young people living in care (Rutter et al, 1998; Newman and Blackburn, 2002a and 2002b; Sinclair et al, 2003). As discussed in Chapter 3, research studies completed on young people leaving care since the beginning of the 1970s show low levels of attainment and participation beyond the minimum school-leaving age. However, as detailed in Chapter 5, good outcomes are associated with placement stability, gender (young women do better than young men, as reflected in national data), a carer committed to helping the young person, and a supportive and encouraging environment for study. This may also include the foster families' own children providing help and acting as role models (Biehal et al, 1995; Department of Health, 2001b; Jackson et al, 2003).

There is also evidence that young people who have had several placements can achieve educational success if they remain in the same school – and this also meant that they were able to maintain friendships and contacts with helpful teachers. Also, late-placed young people who may have experienced a lot of earlier placement disruption, can succeed in foster care, although this was seen by young people and their foster carers as more of a service relationship than a substitute family (Jackson et al, 2003).

Fourth, school or care itself may also provide turning points (Rutter et al, 1998), open the door for participation in a range of leisure or extra-curricular activities that may lead to new friends and opportunities, including the learning of competencies and the development of emotional maturity – and thus promote their resilience (Newman and Blackburn, 2002). Indeed, resilient young people had often been able to turn their negative experiences at home, or in care, into opportunities, with the help of others.

Fifth, preparation for leaving care may also provide young people with opportunities for planning, problem-solving and the learning of new competencies – all resilience-promoting factors (Rutter et al, 1998; Newman and Blackburn, 2002a). As detailed in Chapter 6, this may include the development of self-care skills – personal hygiene, diet and health, including sexual health; practical skills – budgeting, shopping, cooking and cleaning; and interpersonal skills – managing a range of formal and informal relationships. Preparation should be holistic in approach, attaching equal importance to practical, emotional and interpersonal skills – not just, as in the past, practical independence training for young people to manage on their own at the age of 16 plus (Stein and Carey, 1986; Stein and Wade, 2000).

Sixth, many young people leaving care have a compressed and accelerated transition to adulthood which represents a barrier to promoting their resilience. As the discussion of focal theory and transitions suggests, they are denied the psychological opportunity to focus and to deal with changes over time – which is how most young people are able to deal with problems and challenges. Also, they may often be lacking the range and depth of family support of their peers and they may be denied the opportunity to 'space out' – a period of risk-taking, reflection and identity search.

Finally, it has been suggested that the resilience of young people after leaving care is closely associated with their care experience and the support they may receive. In Chapter 5, three outcome groups were identified.

First, the 'moving on' group, who are likely to have had stability and continuity in their lives. They have welcomed the challenge of independent living and gaining more control over their lives – often contrasting this with the restrictions imposed while living in care, including the lack of opportunities to make or participate in decisions which affected their lives. They have seen this as improving their confidence and self-esteem. In general, their resilience has been enhanced by their experiences after care and they have been able to make good use of the help they have been offered, often maintaining contact and support from former carers (Schofield, 2001; Sinclair et al, 2003).

The second group, the 'survivors', had experienced more instability, movement and disruption while living in care than the 'moving on' group. What made the difference to their lives was the personal and professional support they received after leaving care. Specialist leaving care workers, key workers, as well as mentors – the latter identified in the international review as a resilience-promoting factor (Newman and Blackburn, 2002a) and different family members, or some combination of support networks, could help them overcome their very poor starting points at the time of leaving care and thus promote their resilience (Biehal et al, 1995; Clayden and Stein, 2002; Marsh and Peel, 1999).

The third group, the 'victims', was the most disadvantaged group. They had the most damaging pre-care family experiences and, in the main, care was unable to compensate them, to help them overcome their past difficulties. After leaving care they were likely to be unemployed, become homeless and have great difficulties in maintaining their accommodation. They were also highly likely to be lonely, isolated and have mental health problems. Aftercare support was unlikely to be able to help them overcome their very poor starting points and they also lacked or alienated personal support. But it was important to these young people that somebody was there for them.

Key messages

- Four perspectives – attachment theory, focal theory, life course analysis and resilience – offer a way of interpreting the empirical material reviewed in this text.
- To compensate them for their disruption to their early lives many young people require some compensatory 'attachment' or at least stability in their lives – although further movement in care often denies them this.
- At the time of leaving care, too many young people have to cope with major changes in their lives, far younger, and in far less time, than their peers – they are denied the psychological opportunity to 'focus', to deal with changes over time.
- An exploration of the 'life course' of young people leaving care shows how their lives are connected to their biography, their actions and the wider social contexts. Given this complexity, this perspective poses challenges to the simplicity of standardised and separated outcome measures.
- The 'resilience' of young people can be promoted through providing young people with stability, helping them develop a positive sense of identity, enabling a positive experience of education, by having opportunities for turning points, planning and problem-solving, and more gradual and supported transitions from care.
- The resilience of young people is linked to whether they are provided with opportunities to 'move on', 'survive' or remain 'victims'.

8 Conclusion – so what works?

I have argued that different kinds of research knowledge contribute to our under-standing of what works for young people leaving care. To begin with, research is carried out within a context. History, law, policy, as well as social and economic struc-tures provide the backcloth for an exploration of the problems and challenges faced by young people leaving care, the kinds of services they receive and how they are being provided, and what we know about the outcomes of leaving care services. Our knowledge is also derived from evaluations of practice as well as what is often seen as the other end of the spectrum, theory, or more precisely, the links between theoreti-cal and empirical work. Although these different areas have been discussed separate-ly they are closely inter-connected and, ideally, it is through summative knowledge of these different dimensions that we gain a fuller picture of what works.

In the preceding chapters I have reviewed the available research evidence from these areas, and to conclude I am going to summarise what this evidence has shown so that we can gain a better understanding of what works for young people leaving care.

Research in context (Chapter 2) illustrated the complex interplay between ideology, research, law and practice in the making of leaving care policy. The post-war egali-tarian climate, finally signalling the end of the poor law care of children, provided the context for the Children Act 1948 as well as the childcare officer's social casework. New aftercare duties and powers were introduced and this led to the development of specialist services. Also, during this period, young people remained in care until they were 18, the new legal framework mirroring the normative 'rite de passage' of young people at that time. The empirical and theoretical work of Bowlby on maternal dep-rivation and attachment was very influential in the development of social casework and thus in furthering the growth and professional identity of social work – the rise of welfare.

However, ironically, the zenith of welfarism, represented by the reorganisation of personal social services and changes in childcare law introduced in 1971 led, in effect, to the end of specialist aftercare provision. The priority afforded these vulnerable young people lessened, and the age they were expected to leave care reduced to as young as 16. The shifts from a welfare perspective to more radical responses, includ-ing advocacy and a practice increasingly influenced by a developing children's rights discourse proved contradictory. For although supporting the voice and self-organisation of young people, it had little interest in care itself or the fate of care leavers: community work, advocacy and prevention were where it was at. More mainstream developments, including child protection work, planning for permanency, and diversion, by and large ignored care leavers.

From the mid-1970s the findings from researchers were to highlight for the first time the problems faced by young people leaving care, and these findings, combined with sustained campaigning, including the actions and self-organisation of young people themselves and increased awareness by practitioners, provided a momentum for change to the law. The Children Act 1989 was introduced in October 1991, which, although very progressive in many respects, was far weaker in relation to leaving care. Other than a new duty to prepare young people, the Act, in the main, only extended permissive powers.

The 1989 Act was also implemented at the most difficult time for care leavers, with the decline of the traditional job market for young people, shrinking housing options, major cuts in welfare benefits and reduced expenditure on public services. However, the Act did raise the profile of the vulnerability of care leavers and led directly to the introduction of more specialist leaving care schemes. Research carried out during the 1990s highlighted the weakness of the discretionary powers contained within the Act, as well as the complex, inconsistent and discouraging wider social policy framework, particularly in relation to benefits and housing.

It was against this background, as well as the revelations of widespread abuse in children's homes, that the incoming Labour government, elected in 1997, committed itself to legislate for new and stronger duties for care leavers as part of its modernisation programme for children's services. In addition, wider government initiatives to tackle social exclusion were also planned to help care leavers. The Children (Leaving Care) Act was introduced in October 2001. Research carried out during the first two years points to an increased take-up of further education; reductions in those not in education, employment and training; a strengthening of leaving care responsibilities; and improved funding for leaving care teams. However, divisions between better and poorer funded services remained. Also, there is evidence that young people with disabilities, including those in health and educational placements, were being denied access to mainstream leaving care services, as well as concerns that those in 'respite care' are excluded altogether from the provisions of the Act.

What are the *problems and challenges* (Chapter 3) faced by young people leaving care? Early studies, derived in the main from small exploratory qualitative research, described and provided insights into the lives of young people in, and leaving care. They documented their movement and disruption while in care, their poor preparation for leaving and their experiences of loneliness, isolation, homelessness, unstable careers and, often, inadequate assistance after leaving care. However, these early studies, because of their design limitations, were unable to compare the needs of care leavers with other young people.

Research evidence from the 1990s onwards has highlighted key differences between care leavers and other young people: having to be independent at a much younger age, including frequent movement after leaving care and higher levels of homelessness; lower levels of educational attainment and post-16 further and higher education participation rates; higher unemployment rates, unstable career patterns and, linked to this, higher levels of dependency on welfare benefits; earlier parenthood; higher levels of mental health problems and drug use; and higher levels of offending behaviour. Many of these findings are supported by a review of research literature from the United States.

In addition, research studies have also contributed to a greater understanding of specific groups of care leavers. Young parenthood, although often welcomed, brought other difficulties including finding suitable accommodation, personal and financial support. Black and minority ethnic young people, including those of mixed parentage, could experience identity problems derived from a lack of contact with family and community as well as the impact of racism and discrimination. Young unaccompanied refugee and asylum-seeking young people were likely to receive poorer services than other looked-after young people, especially in respect of accommodation and education. Young disabled people could experience inadequate planning and poor consultation, and their transitions from care could be abrupt or delayed by restricted housing and employment options and poor aftercare support.

The evidence from these studies showed that many young people leaving care had to cope with the challenges of major changes in their early lives, and in a far shorter time than other young people. In brief, they had compressed and accelerated transitions to adulthood.

What kinds of *leaving care services* (Chapter 4) have been introduced in response to these needs? Specialist leaving care schemes have developed, particularly since the mid-1980s, to respond to what can be described as the core needs of care leavers – for assistance with accommodation, finance, careers and personal support networks.

In the early literature the main distinctions made were between specialist and non-specialist approaches and between independence and inter-dependence models. Process evaluations completed since the 1990s have identified first, a three-dimensional model for classifying distinctiveness, by differences in service delivery, the nature of the providing agency, and contributions to the development of policy; and second, models of authority-wide provision – a non-specialist service, a centrally organised specialist service, a dispersed specialist service and a centrally organised integrated service. Variations of these models include specialist dual-system arrangements and looked-after adolescent teams. There is also some evidence that a 'corporate parenting case model' has been developed since the introduction of the Children (Leaving Care) Act 2000.

What are *the outcomes of leaving care services?* (Chapter 5). The research findings point to different ways of answering this question.

First, outcome studies showed that specialist leaving care schemes made a positive contribution to specific outcomes for care leavers. They worked particularly well in respect of accommodation and life skills and to some extent in furthering social networks, developing relationships and building self-esteem.

Researching outcomes led to the identification of other influences where schemes worked less well. Successful educational outcomes were closely linked to placement stability, more often although not exclusively achieved in foster care placements, combined with a supportive and encouraging environment for study. And without such stability and encouragement, post-16 employment, education and training outcomes were also likely to be very poor. Success in social networks, personal rela-tionships and in having a positive self-image, although assisted by schemes, was also closely connected with young people having positive, supportive relationships with family members or former foster carers. Stability, continuity, and family and carer links provide the foundation upon which specialist schemes must build if they are to work well.

Second, and adopting a more holistic case approach including taking into account starting points and outcomes, leaving care schemes worked well generally with three-quarters of young people in either achieving good outcomes or making positive progress towards such outcomes in terms of accommodation, means of support, self-esteem and a sense of control over their lives. Research from the United States into preparation programmes highlights the importance of assessment, the need for services to address both 'hard' (practical) and 'soft' (personal) skills, and the importance of targeted services.

Third, young people who go on to higher education are more likely to have had stable care experiences, continuity in their schooling, been encouraged by their birth parents – even though they were unable to care for them – and have been greatly assisted by their foster carers in their schooling.

Fourth, research into the outcomes for young people leaving foster care has identified key variables that distinguish those doing well from those who were less successful: a strong attachment with a family member, partner or partner's family or foster carer was associated with a good outcome. Conversely, those young people who were assessed as disturbed at first contact – and this correlated with other key variables including performance at school, placement disruption and attachment disorder – had poorer outcomes. Another variable, involvement in work, although identified by foster carers as an indication of success, was seen by young people as problematic, especially low-paid, unfulfilling work. Young people being seen as ready and willing to leave was also associated with the 'doing well' outcome measure. In the United States, young people placed with Casey foster carers who did well as adults, were likely to have completed their high school education, attended college or job training, acquired life skills and independent living training, participated in youth clubs or organisations while in care and were less likely to be homeless within one year of leaving care.

Finally, drawing on these different studies, three outcome groups were identified: a 'moving on' group, who achieved a post-care normalising identity; a 'survivors' group, who were just about coping and whose life chances depended on the personal and professional support they received; and a 'victims' group, who were the most disadvantaged group in terms of their pre-care histories, their care experiences and post-care lives.

An exploration of the outcomes of leaving care services contributes to a greater knowledge of the impact of key variables – or in a sense, the bigger picture. But gaining an understanding of how and why interventions might work is more likely to be derived from descriptions and evaluations of *practice* (Chapter 6).

A number of messages can be identified from such evaluations that can guide practice post the Children (Leaving Care) Act. These include: the importance of being committed to, engaging with and involving young people in the decisions that were important to them; working with young people not just for them; being holistic in approach, by attaching equal importance to practical, emotional and interpersonal needs in assessment, planning and practice; identifying formal and informal support networks, including the key role of the personal adviser and leaving care workers as well as family, kinship, friends and mentors; working with other agencies in different ways – housing providers, benefit agencies, education, employment and training agencies and health organisations in meeting the core needs of care leavers; responding to diversity by recognising the needs of different groups of young people, including young men and young women, young lesbian and gay young people, young black and minority ethnic young people, young disabled people, as well as the wide range of individual needs; and by contributing to leaving care policy at the local level, by increasing awareness of issues, contributing to debates and informing policy responses.

Unsurprisingly, perhaps, in such an applied area, there have been few attempts to explore or make explicit theoretical perspectives. Indeed, the 'what works?' movement has been seen by some as anti-theory. In *what works in theory?* (Chapter 7) four different perspectives are discussed.

First, it is suggested that attachment theory is relevant to understanding the experiences of young people whose early family relationships have been disrupted, often by abuse and neglect, and who require some compensatory attachment or stability in their lives. However, many go on to experience further disruption while in care, just the opposite of what they need.

Second, focal theory provides one way of making sense of the accelerated and compressed transitions of young people leaving care – having to cope with major changes in their lives far younger than their peers and in a far shorter time. They are denied the psychological opportunity of focus, of dealing with these major issues over time, that research evidence suggests is how most young people cope well with their journey to adulthood.

Third, life course theory has been used to explore the transitions of young people leaving care. This approach sees young people's lives as an integrated whole linking personal biography, the agency of young people and the wider social contexts.

Ethnographic research, capturing young care leavers' experiences, challenges standardised outcome measures which fail to take into account young people's starting points, as well as the normative assumptions held by social services about achieving independence at 18 years of age. The application of a life course approach to young people's education and careers demonstrates the relationship between pre-care, care and post-care experiences.

Finally, it is argued that the resilience of young people can be promoted through providing stability, helping young people develop a positive sense of identity, have a positive experience of education, have opportunities for turning points, planning and problem-solving in their lives, and more gradual and supported transitions from care. It is suggested that the resilience of young people is linked to whether they are provided with opportunities to 'move on', 'survive', or remain 'victims'.

Research trends and the Children (Leaving Care) Act 2000

What are the implications of the main trends from the research findings, from the early studies to the most recent, for the Children (Leaving Care) Act?

First, the Act, by itself, cannot improve outcomes for young people leaving care. It will have to build upon the foundations of good quality substitute care – the resilience-promoting factors identified above – of which providing stability is critical. But the research evidence from studies completed since the 1970s consistently show the great difficulty in responding to this very basic need for many looked-after young people, over a third experiencing four or more placement moves and only 10 per cent having one move before leaving care.

Second, and linked to the point above, personal advisers under the Act, and specialist leaving care schemes and projects cannot by themselves improve outcomes for care leavers, although they can assist young people, especially after they leave care, as identified in Chapter 4. Their contribution will be closely linked to the quality of substitute care and young people's opportunities for gradual transitions from care. The relationship between care and specialist leaving care provision has been potentially problematic for three reasons since the development of specialist projects during the 1980s.

To begin with, many young people currently move on to accommodation provided by specialist schemes and projects at just 15 or 16 years of age. Not only does this build in additional movement and disruption and accelerate young people's transitions from care, but it also may contribute to the redefinition of foster or residential care – as for young people only up to 15 years of age. Second, there is evidence that preparation for leaving care may be viewed as the responsibility of specialist workers rather than carers, again separating leaving care from ordinary care. Third, the development of specialist leaving care schemes may be seen by authorities as the answer to meeting the needs of care leavers, shifting the focus from the quality of substitute care.

Leaving care should be reclaimed by carers, for, as the research evidence clearly shows, it is they who can provide the stability and continuity young people need during their journey to adulthood. The role of specialist advisers and their teams should not be to take over from them but to assist them in preparing and supporting young people during their transition. Their main role would shift from being a provider of direct care to servicing those who provide care.

Third, the new legal framework provides an opportunity for improving services and thus the level of resourcing for young people leaving care – for example, in terms of housing, finance, careers and personal support – which is very important in assisting them. However, from the 1980s to the implementation of the Act the research evidence reveals a wide degree of variation in the resourcing, range and quality of services between local authorities. The development of benchmarking by the National Leaving Care Advisory Service may help to reduce such inequalities through the publication of service standards, performance indicators and inspection. However, territorial injustices are likely to remain a major challenge, although one way of assessing the impact of the Act could be the reductions in such inequalities.

Fourth, what is also important as well as the quantity is the quality of resource relationships. As the discussion of the 'moving on' group of young people shows, those who had successful transitions out of care not only accessed more resources they also had a lot more interactive relationships. They were, for example, able to *negotiate* decent housing, *derive* meaningful employment or work, participate in community and leisure activities, and *engage* in education. Also, they were able to *participate* in 'general' or open access community activities and opportunities as distinct from 'specialist' leaving care provision – although the latter can often pave the way for the former. There is a lot of practice evidence from the 1980s onwards showing that leaving care services have played a major role in involving young people at different levels: policy consultation, training as well as in individual practice. The Act should continue this momentum. But on a more cautionary note, there is a balance to be achieved between young people's rights to participation through greater involvement and meeting their emotional and developmental needs. Neither a shallow and token legalism which rejects all needs in favour of rights or a crude and narrow pathologising which reduces young people to receptacles of professionally defined need, will serve these young people well.

Fifth, not all groups of young people are benefiting equally under the Act. There is research evidence that young disabled people are being denied access to mainstream leaving care services partly as a consequence of poor communication between disabilities teams, leaving care services and adult services. Also some young unaccompanied asylum-seeking young people may be excluded from the Act if they are being supported under Section 17 of the Children Act 1989 instead of being accommodated. The specific needs of groups of care leavers could also be given more prominence: the racism experienced by minority ethnic young people; the lack of support for young parents, in their own right, not just as an extension of child protection concerns; and the mental health of young care leavers. There has been, albeit more recently, research evidence of the mental health problems of looked-after young people. For most of these young people they will be associated with their damaging pre-care experiences within their families. These mental health problems are likely to have contributed to the reasons for them coming into care in the first place as well as being associated with poor outcomes after care. These connections, as with education, demonstrate the need for interventions across the life course of young people and their families, to address problems within families when they arise, to improve the quality of care and provide skilled help for young people after they leave care.

Finally, a connecting theme arising from the body of research findings discussed in this volume is that leaving care should be at one with a common developmental journey, from being a young person to becoming an adult. Those looked-after young people who experienced such a common journey are the most likely to find fulfilment in their careers and personal lives and overcome the damaging consequences of familial problems, abuse or neglect. They are able to become more independent not in an emotionally isolated way, but to 'move on' from care into education, employment or parenthood and thus achieve an 'ordinary' or 'common' identity – not just coping as 'survivors', or, as too many young people are, trapped within welfare identities as 'victims'.

References

Action on Aftercare Consortium, Barnardo's (1996) *Too much too young; the failure of social policy in meeting the needs of care leavers.* Barnardo's, Barkingside.

Ainsworth, MDS, Eichberg, C (1991) Effects on infant mother attachment of mother's unresolved loss of an attachment figure, or other traumatic experience. In Parkes, CM, Stevenson-Hinde, J, Marris, P (eds) *Attachment across the life cycle.* Routledge, London.

Aldgate, J, Heath, A, Colton, M, Simm, M (1993) Social work and the education of children in foster care. *Adoption and Fostering* 17(3): 25–34.

Allard, AS (2002) *A case study investigation into the implementation of the Children (Leaving Care) Act 2000.* NCH, London.

Allen, M (2003) *Into the mainstream: care leavers entering work, education and training.* Joseph Rowntree Foundation, York.

Anderson, I, Quilgars, D (1995) *Foyers for young people: evaluation of a pilot initiative.* Centre for Housing Policy, University of York.

Arden, N (1977) *Child of a system.* Quartet Books, London.

Audit Commission (2000) *Another country: implementing dispersal under the immigration and Asylum Act 1999.* Audit Commission, London.

Aycotte, W, Williamson, L (2001) *Separated children in the United Kingdom: an overview of the current situation.* Refugee Council and Save the Children, London.

BAAF, Refugee Council (2001) *Where are the children? A mapping exercise on numbers of unaccompanied asylum-seeking children in the UK.* BAAF and Refugee Council, London.

Baldwin, D (1998) *Growing up in and out of care: an ethnographic approach to young people's transitions to adulthood.* PhD Thesis, University of York Library, York.

Banks, M, Bates, I, Breakwell, G, Bynner, J, Emler, N, Jamieson, L, Roberts, K (1992) *Careers and identities.* Open University Press, Buckingham.

Barn, R (1993) *Black children in the public care system*. Batsford, London.

Barn, R, Sinclair, R, Ferdinand, D (1997) *Acting on principle: an examination of race and ethnicity in social services provision to children and families*. BAAF, London.

Barn, R, Andrew, L, Mantovani, N (2004) *Life after care: a study of young people from different ethnic groups*. Joseph Rowntree Foundation, York.

Barnardo's (1987) *Developments in childcare*. Film Script, Barnardo's, Barkingside.

Barnardo's (1989) *I can't go back to mum and dad*. Barnardo's, Barkingside.

Barnardo's (2000) *Children first and foremost: meeting the needs of unaccompanied asylum-seeking children*. Survey findings presented at Barnardo's seminar, 4 July 2002.

Bean, P, Melville, J (1989) *Lost children of the empire*. Unwin Hyman, London.

Bebbington, A, Miles, J (1989) The background of children who enter local authority care. *British Journal of Social Work* 19(5): 349–368.

Beck, U (1992) *Risk society: towards a new modernity*. Sage, London.

Beresford, B, Sloper, P, Baldwin, S, Newman, T (1996) *What works in services for families with a disabled child?* Barnardo's, Barkingside.

Berridge, D, Brodie, I (1998) *Children's homes revisited*. Jessica Kingsley, London.

Biehal, N, Clayden, J, Stein, M, Wade, J (1992) *Prepared for living? A survey of young people leaving the care of three local authorities*. National Children's Bureau, London.

Biehal, N, Clayden, J, Stein, M, Wade, J (1995) *Moving on: young people and leaving care schemes*. HMSO, London.

Biehal, N, Wade, J (1996) Looking back, looking forward: care leavers, families and change. *Children and Youth Services Review* 18(4/5): 425–445.

Biehal, N, Wade, J (1999) 'I thought it would be easy': the early housing careers of young people leaving care. In Rugg, J (ed) *Young people, housing and social policy*. Routledge, London.

Black and In Care (1984) *Black and in care conference report*. Children's Legal Centre, London.

Black, N (1996) Why we need observational studies to evaluate the effectiveness of health care. *British Medical Journal* 312, 1215–1218.

Bohman, M, Sigvardsson, S (1980) Negative social heritage. *Adoption and Fostering* 101 (3): 25–34

Bonnerjea, L (1990) *Leaving care in London*. London Boroughs' Children's Regional Planning Committee, London.

Bowlby, J (1973) *Attachment and Loss*, Vol. 2. *Separation: anxiety and anger*. Hogarth, London.

Bowlby, J (1982a; first published 1969) *Attachment and Loss*, Vol. 1. *Attachment*. Hogarth, London.

Bowlby, J (1982b) *Attachment and Loss*, Vol. 3. *Loss: sadness and depression*. Hogarth, London.

Bretherton, I (1991) Roots and growing points in attachment theory. In Parkes, CM, Stevenson-Hinde, J, Marris, P (eds) *Attachment across the life cycle*. Routledge, London.

Broad, B (1994) *Leaving care in the 1990's: the results of a national survey*. Royal Philanthropic Society, Westerham.

Broad, B (1998) *Young people leaving care, life after the Children Act 1989*. Jessica Kingsley, London.

Broad, B (1999) Young people leaving care: moving towards 'joined up' solutions? *Children and Society* 13(2): 81–93.

Broad, B (2003) *After the Act: implementing the Children (Leaving Care) Act 2000*. Action on Aftercare Consortium and De Montfort University, Leicester.

Burgess, C (1981) *In care and into work*. Tavistock, London.

Cashmore, J, Paxman, M (1996) *Wards leaving care: a longitudinal study*. NSW Department of Community Services, Sydney, New South Wales.

Chase, E, Knight, A, Warwick, I, Aggleton, P (2003a) *Teenage pregnancy and young people in and leaving local authority care: determinants and support*, Report for the Department of Health. Thomas Coram Research Unit, London.

Chase, E, Knight, A, Warwick, I, Aggleton, P (2003b) *Pregnancy and parenthood among young people in and leaving local authority care*, Report for the Department of Health. Thomas Coram Research Unit, London.

Cheesbrough, S (2002) *The educational attainment of people who have been in care: findings from the 1970 British cohort study* (www.socialexclusionunit.gov.uk)

Cheetham, J, Fuller, R, Petch, A, McIvor, R (1992) *Evaluating social work effectiveness*. Open University Press, Buckingham.

Cheung, SY, Buchanan, A (1997) Malaise scores in adulthood of children and young people who have been in care. *Journal of Child Psychology and Psychiatry* 38 (5): 575–580.

Cheung, SY, Heath, A (1994) After care: the education and occupation of adults who have been in care. *Oxford Review of Education* 20(3): 361–374.

Clarke, J (1996) After social work. In Parton, N (ed) *Social theory, social change and social work*. Routledge, London.

Clayden, J (2003) *Coram education service evaluation*. SWRDU, University of York, York.

Clayden, J, Stein, M (1996) Self-care skills and becoming an adult. In Jackson, S and Kilroe, S (eds) *Looking after children, good parenting, good outcomes, Reader.* HMSO, London.

Clayden, J, Stein, M (2002) *Mentoring for care leavers, evaluation report.* Prince's Trust, London.

Coleman, JC (1974) *Relationships in adolescence*. Routledge and Kegan Paul, London.

Coleman, JC (1978) Current contradictions in adolescent theory. *Journal of Youth and Adolescence* 7: 131–141.

Coleman, JC (ed) (1979) *The school years*. Methuen, London.

Coleman, JC (1980) Friendship and the peer group in adolescence. In Alderson, J (ed) *Handbook of adolescent psychology*. John Wiley, New York.

Coleman, JC, Hendry, L (1999) *The nature of adolescence*. Routledge, London.

Coles, B (1995) *Youth and social policy*. UCL Press, London.

Collins, S, Stein, M (1989) Users fight back: collectives in social work. In Rojeck, C, Peacock, G, Collins, S (eds) *The haunt of misery*. Routledge, London.

Colton, M (2002) Factors associated with abuse in residential childcare institutions. *Children and Society* 16(1): 33–44.

Cook, JR (1994) Are we helping foster care youth prepare for their future? *Children and Youth Services Review* 16(3/4): 213–229.

Corlyon, J, McGuire, C (1997) *Pregnancy and parenthood: the views and experiences of young people in public care*. National Children's Bureau, London.

Courtney, ME, Piliavan, I, Grogan-Kayor, A, Nesmith, A (2001) Foster youth transitions to adulthood: a longitudinal view of youth leaving care. *Child Welfare* 6: 685–717.

Courtney, ME, Terao, S (2002) *Classification of independent living services*. Chapin Hall Center for Children at the University of Chicago, Chicago.

Courtney, ME, Hughes, D (2003) *The transition to adulthood for youth 'aging out' of the foster care system*. Chapin Hall Center for Children at the University of Chicago, Chicago.

Craig, T (1996) *Off to a bad start*. Mental Health Foundation, London.

Crittenden, PM (1992) Children's strategies for coping with abuse and neglect: an interpretation using attachment theory. *Child Abuse and Neglect* 16: 329–343.

Dean, J (2003) *Disabled young adults and the parental home*, Findings 973. Joseph Rowntree Foundation, York.

Dennis, J (2002) *A case for change: how refugee children in England are missing out*. The Children's Society, Refugee Council and Save the Children, London.

Department for Education and Skills (2003) *Statistics for education: care leavers, 2002–2003, England*. HMSO, London.

Department for Education and Skills (2004) *Children looked after by local authorities, year ending 31 March 2003*. HMSO, London.

Department of the Environment (1981) *Single and homeless*. HMSO, London.

Department of Health (1991a) *Looking after children: a guide to the action and assessment schedules*. HMSO, London.

Department of Health (1991b) *The Children Act 1989, guidance and regulations*, Vol. 4. HMSO, London.

Department of Health (1991c) *Children in the public care*. HMSO, London.

Department of Health (1997) *When leaving home is also leaving care: an inspection of services for young people leaving care*, Social Services Inspectorate. DoH, London (http://www.dfes.gov.uk/rsgateway/DB/VOL/v000454/index.shtml).

Department of Health (1998) *Quality protects: framework for action*. DoH, London.

Department of Health (1999) *Adoption now: messages from research*. DoH, London.

Department of Health (1999) *Me, survive, out there? New arrangements for young people living in and leaving care*. DoH, London.

Department of Health (2001a) *Children (Leaving Care) Act 2000; regulations and guidance*. DoH, London.

Department of Health (2001b) *Children Act report 2000*. DoH, London.

Department of Health/Centrepoint (2002) *Care leaving strategies: a good practice handbook*. DoH, London.

Department of Health (2003a) *Outcome indicators for looked after children*. DoH, London.

Department of Health (2003b) *Guidance on accommodating children in need and their families, LAC (2003) 13*. DoH, London.

Department of Health (2003c) *Outcome indicators for looked after children, twelve months to 30 September 2002*. DoH, London.

Dixon, J, Stein, M (2002) *A study of throughcare and aftercare services in Scotland.* Scotland's Children, Children (Scotland) Act 1995, Research Findings No. 3. Scottish Executive, Edinburgh.

Dixon, J, Stein, M (2003) Leaving care in Scotland: the residential experience. *Scottish Journal of Residential Child Care* 2(2): 7–16.

Dixon, J, Lee, J, Wade, J, Byford, S, Weatherly, H (2004) *Young people leaving care: an evaluation of costs and outcomes,* Report to the DfES, University Of York, York.

Donzelot, J (1980) *The policing of families.* Hutchinson, London.

Dorman, M (1992) 'Witness tells of systematic beatings', Evidence to the Leicestershire Inquiry, *Leicester Mercury*, 20 February 1992, p8.

Downes, C (1992) *Separation revisited.* Ashgate, Aldershot.

Doyal, L, Gough, I (1984) A theory of human needs. *Critical Social Policy* 10: 6–38.

Doyle, P (1989) *The God squad.* Corgi Books, London.

Dumaret, AC, Coppel-Batsch, M, Courand, S (1997) Adult outcome of children reared for long-term periods in foster families. *Child Abuse and Neglect* 20: 911–927.

Elmer, N (2001) *Self-esteem, the costs and causes of low self worth.* Joseph Rowntree Foundation, York.

Farmer, E, Pollock, S (1997) *Substitute care for sexually abused and abusing children,* Report to the Department of Health. School for Policy Studies, University of Bristol, Bristol.

Festinger, T (1983) *No one ever asked us: a postscript to foster care.* Columbia University Press, New York.

Fever, F (1994) *Who cares?* Warner, London.

First Key (1987) *A study of black young people leaving care.* First Key, Leeds.

First Key (1992) *A study of black young people leaving care.* First Key, Leeds.

First Key (1992) *A survey of local authority provision for young people leaving care.* First Key, Leeds.

First Key (1996) *Standards in leaving care.* First Key, Leeds.

Fisher, M (ed) (1983) *Speaking of clients.* Joint Unit for Social Services Research/Community Care, University of Sheffield, Sheffield.

Fraser, D (1976) *The evolution of the British welfare state.* Macmillan, London.

Frost, N, Stein, M (1989) *The politics of child welfare.* Harvester Wheatsheaf, Hemel Hempstead.

Frost, N, Stein, M (1995) *Working with young people leaving care.* HMSO, London.

Fry, E (1992) *After care: making the most of foster care.* NFCA, London.

Garmzey, N (1987) Stress, competence and development: continuities in the study of schizophrenic adults, children vulnerable to psychopathology, and the search for stress resistant children. *American Journal of Orthopsychiatry* 57: 159–174.

Garnett, L (1992) *Leaving care and after.* National Children's Bureau, London.

Giddens, A (1991) *Modernity and self-identity: self and society in the late modern age.* Polity Press, Cambridge.

Gilligan, R (2001) *Promoting resilience: a resource guide on working with children in the care system.* BAAF, London.

Godek, S (1976) *Leaving care.* Barnardo's, Barkingside.

Graham, J, Bowling, B (1995) *Young people and crime.* Home Office Research and Planning Unit, London.

Greim, P (1995) Summary of public/private ventures' investigations of adult/youth relationship programs. In Mech, VE, Rycraft, JR (eds) *Preparing foster youths for adult living: proceedings of an invitational research conference.* Child Welfare League of America, Washington.

Hahn, A (1994) The use of assessment procedure in foster care to evaluate readiness for independent living. *Children and Youth Services Review* 16(3/4): 171–179.

Hai, N, Williams, A (2004) *Implementing the Children (Leaving Care) Act 2000, the experience of eight London boroughs.* National Children's Bureau, London.

Hall, S (1992) The question of cultural identity. In Hall, S, Held, D, McGrew, T (eds) *Modernity and its futures.* Polity Press, Cambridge.

Harding, L (2001) *Platform, rollercoaster.* Zinc Arts Projects, Yarm, Stockton on Tees.

Harris, J, Rabiee, P, Priestley, M (2002) Enabled by the Act? The reframing of aftercare services for young disabled. In Wheal, A (ed) *The RHP companion to leaving care.* Russell House Publishing, Lyme Regis.

Hart, A (1984) Resources for transitions from care. In *Leaving care – where?* Conference Report. National Association of Young People in Care, London.

Haydon, D (2003) *Teenage pregnancy and looked after children/care leavers: a resource for teenage pregnancy co-ordinators.* Barnardo's, Barkingside.

Hazel, N, Hagell, A, Liddle, M, Archer, D, Grimshaw, R, King, J (2000) *Detention and training: assessment of the detention and training order and its impact on the secure estate across England and Wales.* Youth Justice Board, London.

Heath, A, Colton, M, Aldgate, J (1989) The educational progress of children in and out of foster care. *British Journal of Social Work* 19: 447–460.

Hendry, LB, Shucksmith, J, McCrae, J (1985) *Young people's leisure and lifestyles in modern Scotland.* Department of Education, University of Aberdeen and Scottish Sports Council, Edinburgh.

Heywood, J (1978) *Children in care.* Routledge and Kegan Paul, London.

Hirst, M, Baldwin, S (1994) *Unequal opportunities: growing up disabled.* HMSO, London.

Hitchman, J (1966) *The King of the Barbereens.* Penguin Books, London.

Hobcraft, J (1998) *Intergenerational and life-course transmission of social exclusion: influences of childhood poverty, family disruption and contact with the police.* CASE Paper 15. London School of Economics, London.

Horrocks, C (2002) Using life course theory to explore the social and developmental pathways of young people leaving care. *Journal of Youth Studies* 5(3): 325–335.

House of Commons (1968) *Report of the committee on local authority and allied personal social services*, Cmnd 9703. HMSO, London.

House of Commons (1984) *Second report from the social services committee, children in care.* HMSO, London.

House of Commons (2000) *Lost in care: Report of the tribunal of inquiry into the abuse of children in care in the former county council areas of Gwynedd and Cllwyd since 1974.* The Stationery Office, London.

Howe, D (1995) *Attachment theory for social work practice.* Macmillan, London.

Hutson, S (1995) *Care leavers and young homeless people in Wales: the exchange of good practice.* University of Wales, Swansea.

Hutson, S (1997) *Supported housing: the experience of young care leavers.* Barnardo's, Barkingside.

Hutson, S, Liddiard, M (1994) *Youth homelessness: the construction of a social issue.* Macmillan, London.

Iglehart, AP (1994) Adolescents in foster care: predicting readiness for independent living. *Children and Youth Services Review* 16(3/4): 159–168.

Iglehart, AP (1995) Readiness for independence: comparison of foster care, kinship care, and non-foster care adolescents. *Children and Youth Services Review* 17(3): 417–432.

Ince, L (1998) *Making it alone: a study of the care experiences of young black people.* BAAF, London.

Ince, L (1999) Preparing black young people leaving care. In Barn, R, *Working with black children and adolescents in need.* BAAF, London.

Jackson, S (1988–89) Residential care and education. *Children and Society* 4: 335–350.

Jackson, S (1994) Educating children in residential and foster care. *Oxford Review of Education* 20(3): 267–279.

Jackson, S (ed) (2001) *Nobody ever told us school mattered; raising the educational attainment of children in care.* BAAF, London

Jackson, S (2002) Promoting stability and continuity of care away from home. In McNeish, D, Newman, T, Roberts, H (eds) *What works for children?* Open University Press, Buckingham.

Jackson, S, Thomas, N (2001) *What works in creating stability for looked after children?* Barnardo's, Barkingside.

Jackson, S, Ajayi, S, Quigley, M (2003) *By degrees: the first year, from care to university.* The Frank Buttle Trust, London.

Jones, G, Wallace, C (1992) *Youth, family and citizenship.* Open University Press, Buckingham.

Jones, G (2002) *The youth divide: diverging paths to adulthood.* Foundations, Joseph Rowntree Foundation, York.

Kahan, B (1979) *Growing up in care.* Blackwell, Oxford.

Kelleher, P, Kelleher, C, Corbett, M (2000) *Left out on their own, young people leaving care in Ireland.* Focus Ireland, Dublin.

Kidane, S (2002) Asylum seeking and refugee children in the UK. In Wheal, A (ed) *The RHP companion to leaving care.* Russell House Publishing, Lyme Regis.

Kiernan, K (1992) The impact of family disruption in childhood on transitions made in young adult life. *Population Studies* 46: 213–34.

Kiernan, K, Wicks, M (1990) *Family change and future policy.* Joseph Rowntree Foundation/Family Policy Studies Centre, York.

Kirby, P (1994) *A word from the street.* Centrepoint, London.

Knapp, M (1989) *Measuring childcare outcomes*, PSSRU Discussion Paper 630. University of Kent, Canterbury.

Kohli, R, Mather, R (2003) Promoting psychosocial well-being in unaccompanied young asylum seekers. *Child & Family Social Work* 8(3): 201–212.

Koprowska, J, Stein, M (2000) The mental health of 'looked after' young people. In Aggleton, P, Hurry, J, Warwick, I, (eds) *Young people and mental health.* Wiley, Chichester.

Kroger, J (1985) Relationships during adolescence: a cross national comparison of New Zealand and United States teenagers. *Journal of Youth and Adolescence* 8: 47–56.

Kufeldt, K, Simard, M, Tite, R, Vachon, J (2003) The looking after children in Canada project: educational outcomes. In Kufeldt, K, McKenzie, B (eds) *Child welfare, connecting research, policy and practice.* Wilfrid Laurier University Press, Ontario, Canada.

Levy, A, Kahan, B (1991) *The pindown experience and the protection of children: the report of the Staffordshire childcare inquiry.* Staffordshire County Council, Stoke.

Lupton, C (1985) *Moving out.* Portsmouth Polytechnic, Portsmouth.

Luthar, S, Cicchetti, D, Becker, B (2000) The construct of resilience: a critical evaluation and guidelines for future work. *Child Development* 71(3): 543–562.

Lynes, D, Goddard, J (1995) *The view from the front.* Norfolk County Council Social Services Department, Norwich.

Macdonald, G, Roberts, H (1995) *What works in the early years? Effective interventions for children and their families in health, social welfare, education and child protection.* Barnardo's, Barkingside.

MacVeigh, J (1982) *Gaskin.* Jonathan Cape, London.

Maluccio, AN, Kreiger, R, Pine, BA (eds) (1990) *Preparing adolescents for life after foster care.* Child Welfare League of America, Washington.

Markey, K (1998) 'Somewhere to call home'. *The Big Issue in the North*, March 2001: 16–22.

Marsh, P, Peel, M (1999) *Leaving care in partnership: family involvement with care leavers.* The Stationery Office, London.

Maslow, A (1970) *Motivation and personality.* Harper and Row, New York.

Mayer, J, Timms, N (1970) *The client speaks.* Routledge and Kegan Paul, London.

McCann, JB, James, A, Wilson, S, Dunn, G (1996) Prevalence of psychiatric disorders in young people in the care system. *British Medical Journal* 3313: 1529–1530.

McCluskey, J (1994) *Acting in isolation: an evaluation of the effectiveness of the Children Act for young homeless people.* CHAR, London.

McCord, J, McCord, W, Thurber, E (1960) The effects of foster home placement in the prevention of adult anti-social behaviour. *Social Services Review* 34: 415–419.

McDonald, TP, Allen, RI, Westerfielt, A, Piliavan, I (1996) *Assessing the long-term effects of foster care: a research synthesis.* Child Welfare League of America, Washington.

McParlin, P (1996) *The education of young people looked after.* First Key, Leeds.

Mech, VE (1994) Preparing foster youth for adulthood: a knowledge building perspective. *Children and Youth Services Review* 16(3/4): 141–145.

Mech, VE, Ludy-Dobson, C, Hulseman, FS (1994) Life skills knowledge: a survey of foster adolescents in three placement settings. *Children and Youth Services Review* 16(3/4): 181–200.

Mech, VE, Rycraft, JR (eds) (1995) *Preparing foster youths for adult living: proceedings of an invitational research conference.* Child Welfare League of America, Washington.

Meier, E (1965) Current circumstances in former foster children. *Child Welfare* 44: 196–206.

Melzer, H, Gatward, R, Goodman, R, Ford, T (2000) *Mental health of children and adolescents in Great Britain.* The Stationery Office, London.

Melzer, H, Corbin, T, Gatward, R, Goodman, R, Ford, T (2003) *The mental health of young people looked after by local authorities in England.* National Statistics, London.

Menmuir, R (1994) Involving residential social workers and foster carers in reading with young people in their care: the PRAISE reading project. *Oxford Review of Education* 20(3): 329–338.

Milham, S, Bullock, R, Hosie, K, Haak, M (1986) *Lost in care.* Gower, Aldershot.

Mitchell, F (2003) The social services response to unaccompanied children in England. *Child & Family Social Work* 8(3): 179–190.

Morgan-Klein, B (1985) *Where am I going to stay?* Scottish Council for Single Homeless, Edinburgh.

Morris, J (1995) *Going missing? A research and policy review of disabled children and young people living away from their families.* Who Cares? Trust, London.

Morris, J (1998) *Still missing? The experiences of disabled children and young people living away from their families.* Who Cares? Trust, London.

Morris, J (1999) *Move on up: supporting young disabled people in their transitions to adulthood.* Barnardo's, Barkingside.

Mulvey, T (1977) Aftercare – who cares? *Concern*, No. 26. National Children's Bureau, London.

Newburn, T, Ward, J, Pearson, G (2002) *Drug use among young people in care*, Research Briefing, 7. Economic and Social Research Council, Swindon.

Newman, T, Blackburn, S (2002a) *Transitions in the lives of children and young people: resilience factors*, Interchange 78. Scottish Executive, Edinburgh.

Newman, T, Blackburn, S (2002b) *Transitions in the lives of children and young people: resilience factors*, Report for the Scottish Executive education and young people research unit, Edinburgh (www.scotland.gov.uk /library5/education/ic78-00.asp).

NHS Scotland (2000) *Scottish health statistics 2000.* Information and Statistics Division, Edinburgh.

Owusu-Bempah, J (1994) Race, self-identity and social work. *British Journal of Social Work* 24: 123–136.

Packman, J (1981) *The child's generation.* Blackwell and Robertson, London.

Page, R, Clark, G (eds) (1977) *Who cares? Young people in care speak out.* National Children's Bureau, London.

Parker, R, Ward, H, Jackson, S, Aldgate, J, Wedge, P (eds) (1991) *Assessing outcomes in childcare.* HMSO, London.

Parr, J (1980) *Labouring children: British immigrant apprentices in Canada 1869-1924.* Croom Helm, London.

Parton, N (1985) *The politics of child abuse.* Macmillan, London.

Pawson, R, Barnes, C, Boaz, A, Grayson, L, Long, A (2003) *Types and quality of social care knowledge stage one: a classification of types of social care knowledge.* UK Centre for Evidence Based Policy and Practice, Working Paper 17. Economic and Social Research Council, Swindon.

Pearson, G (1975) *The deviant imagination.* Macmillan, London.

Pecora, PJ, Williams, J, Kessler, RJ, Downs, A, O'Brien, K, Hiripi, E, Moorello, S (2004) *Assessing the effects of foster care: early results from the Casey national alumni study.* Casey Family Programs, Seattle, WA (http://www.casey.org).

Phoenix, A (1991) *Young mothers.* Polity Press, Cambridge.

Pinkerton, J, McCrea, J (1999) *Meeting the challenge? Young people leaving care in Northern Ireland.* Ashgate, Aldershot.

Prasad R (2003) No longer cast adrift. *The Guardian, Society*, 17 September 2003.

Priestley, M, Rabiee, P, Harris, J (2003) Young disabled people and the 'new arrangements' for leaving care in England and Wales. *Children and Youth Services Review* 25(11): 863–890.

Prison Reform Trust (1991) *The identikit prisoner.* Prison Reform Trust, London.

Quinton, D, Rutter, M, Liddle, C (1984) Institutional rearing, parenting difficulties and marital support. *Psychological Medicine* 14: 107–124.

Rabiee, P, Priestley, M, Knowles, J (2001) *Whatever next? Young disabled people leaving care.* First Key, Leeds.

Ramsey, M, Percy, A (1996) *Drug misuse declared: results of the 1994 British crime survey*, Home Office Research Study 151. Home Office, London.

Randall, G (1988) *No way home.* Centrepoint, London.

Randall, G (1989) *Homeless and hungry.* Centrepoint, London.

Raychuba, B (1987) *Report on the special needs of youth in the care of the child welfare system.* National Youth In Care Network, Ontario.

Ridley, J, McCluskey, S (2003) Exploring the perceptions of young people in care and care leavers of their health needs. *Scottish Journal of Residential Child Care* 12(1).

Rowe, J, Hundleby, M, Garnett, L (1989) *Childcare now*. Batsford/BAAF, London.

Rutter, M (1985) Resilience in the face of adversity: protective factors and resistance to psychiatric disorders. *British Journal of Psychiatry* 147: 589–611.

Rutter, M (1987) Psychosocial resilience and protective mechanisms. *American Journal of Orthopsychiatry* 57: 316–331.

Rutter, M (1999) Resilience concepts and findings: implications for family therapy. *Journal of Family Therapy* 21: 119–144.

Rutter, M, Giller, H, Hagell, A (1998) *Antisocial behaviour by young people*. Cambridge University Press, Cambridge.

Saunders, L, Broad, B (1997) *The health needs of young people leaving care*. De Montfort University, Leicester.

Schofield, G (2001) Resilience and family placement: a lifespan perspective, *Adoption and Fostering* 25(3): 6–19.

Scottish Council for Single Homeless (1981) *Think single*. SCSH, Edinburgh.

Scottish Health Feedback (2001) *A study of the health needs of young people with experience of being in care in Glasgow*. The Big Step, Glasgow.

Scottish Health Feedback (2003) *The health needs and issues of young people from Glasgow living in foster care settings*. The Big Step, Glasgow.

Sharpe, S (1987) *Falling for love: teenage mothers talk*. Virago, London.

Shaw, C (1998) *Remember my messages: the experiences and views of 200 children in public care*. Who Cares? Trust, London.

Shaw, I, Gould, N (2001) *Qualitative research in social work*. Sage, London.

Simmonds, R, Blythe, DA (1987) *Moving into adolescence*. Aldine de Gruyter, New York.

Sinclair, I (2000) 'Methods and measurement in evaluative social work' paper from ESRC seminar series Theorising Social Work Research, NISW (www.nisw.org.uk/tsivr/sinclair.htmi)

Sinclair, I, Gibbs, I (1998) *Children's homes: a study in diversity*. Wiley, Chichester.

Sinclair, I, Baker, C, Wilson, K, Gibbs, I (2003) *What happens to foster children?* Report to the Department of Health. University of York, York.

Sinclair, R, Garnett, L, Berridge, D (1995) *Social work and assessment with adolescents*. National Children's Bureau, London.

Sissay, L (1984) A life less ordinary. *Who Cares?* 60

Skuse, T, Ward, H (2004) *Children's views of care and accommodation*, Report to the Department of Health. Centre for Child and Family Research, Loughborough University, Loughborough.

Smit, M (1995) Preparation for discharge from residential care: a report from the Netherlands. In Mech, VE, Rycraft, JR (eds) *Preparing foster youths for adult living*. Child Welfare League of America, Washington.

Smith, C (ed) (1994) *Partnership in action: developing effective aftercare projects*. Royal Philanthropic Society, Westerham.

Smith, P (1989) *The Children Act 1989*, Highlight. National Children's Bureau, London.

Social Exclusion Unit (1998a) *Rough sleeping*. The Stationery Office, London.

Social Exclusion Unit (1998b) *Truancy and social exclusion*. The Stationery Office, London.

Social Exclusion Unit (1999) *Teenage pregnancy*. The Stationery Office, London.

Social Exclusion Unit (2003) *A better education for children in care*. The Stationery Office, London.

St Clair, L, Osborn, AF (1987) The ability and behaviour of children who have been in care or separated from their parents. *Early Child Development and Care* 28(3) Special Issue.

Stein, E, Raegrant, N, Ackland, S, Avison, W (1994) Psychiatric disorders of children in care: methodology and demographic correlates. *Canadian Journal of Psychiatry* 39: 341–347.

Stein, M (1983) Protest in care. In Jordan, B, Parton, N (eds) *The political dimensions of social work*. Blackwell, Oxford.

Stein, M (1990) *Living out of care*. Barnardo's, Barkingside.

Stein, M (1991) *Leaving care and the 1989 Children Act, the agenda*. First Key, Leeds.

Stein, M (1993) The abuses and uses of residential childcare. In Ferguson, H, Gilligan, R, Torode, R (eds) *Surviving childhood adversity*. Social Studies Press, Dublin.

Stein, M (1994) Leaving care, education and career trajectories. *Oxford Review of Education* 20(3): 349–360.

Stein, M (1997) *What works in leaving care?* Barnardo's, Barkingside.

Stein, M (1999) Leaving care: reflections and challenges. In Stevenson, O (ed) *Child welfare in the UK*. Blackwell, Oxford.

Stein, M (forthcoming) *Overcoming the odds; resilience and young people leaving care*. Joseph Rowntree Foundation, York.

Stein, M, Carey, K (1986) *Leaving care*. Blackwell, Oxford.

Stein, M, Ellis, S (1983) *Gizza say, reviews and young people in care*. NAYPIC, London.

Stein, M, Maynard, C (1985) *I've never been so lonely*. NAYPIC, London.

Stein, M, Pinkerton, J, Kelleher, P (2000) Young people leaving care in England, Northern Ireland, and Ireland. *European Journal of Social Work* 3(3): 235–46.

Stein, M, Wade, J (2000) *Helping care leavers: problems and strategic responses*. DoH, London.

Stone, M (1990) *Young people leaving care*. Royal Philanthropic Society, Westerham.

Strathdee, R (1992) *No way back*. Centrepoint, London.

Strathdee, R, Johnson, M (1994) *Out of care and on the streets, young people, care leavers and homelessness.* Centrepoint, London.

Such, C, Utting, W, Lambert, L (1981) *Out of care, come of age.* National Children's Bureau, London.

Taylor, C (2003) 'Social work and looked after children'. In Smith, DB (ed) *Evidenced-based practice.* Jessica Kingsley, London.

The Big Issue (2001) *10th birthday survey*, September 2000.

Timms, N (1973) *Receiving end, consumer accounts of social help of children.* Routledge, London.

Tizard, B, Phoenix, A (1993) *Black, white or mixed race?* Routledge, London.

Triseliotis, J (1980) Growing up in foster care. In Triseliotis, J (ed) *New developments in foster care and adoption.* Routledge and Kegan Paul, London.

Triseliotis, J, Russell, J (1984) *Hard to place.* Heinemann, London.

Triseliotis, J, Borland, M, Hill, M, Lambert, L (1995) *Teenagers and social work services.* HMSO, London.

Utting, W (1991) *Children in public care: a review of residential childcare.* HMSO, London

Utting, W (1997) *People like us: the report of the review of the safeguards for children living away from home.* HMSO, London.

Van Der Waals (1960) Former foster children reflect on their childhood. *Children* 7: 29–33.

Vernon, J (2000) *Audit and assessment of leaving care services in London.* National Children's Bureau, London.

Wade, J (1997) Developing leaving care services: tapping the potential of foster carers. *Adoption and Fostering* 21(3): 40–49.

Wade, J (2003) *Leaving care.* Quality Protects Research Briefing.

Wade, J, Biehal, N, Clayden, J, Stein, M (1998) *Going missing: young people absent from care.* Wiley, Chichester.

Wakefield Accommodation Project (1996) *Annual Report, 1995–1996.* Barnardo's, Wakefield, City of Wakefield MDC.

Waldinger, G, Furman, WM (1994) Two models of preparing youths for emancipation. *Children and Youth Services Review* 16(3/4): 201–212.

Walker, TG (1994) Educating children in public care: a strategic approach, *Oxford Review of Education* 20(3): 39–48.

Walker, M (2002) Risk, Opportunity and Leaving Care. In Wheal, A (ed) *The RHP Companion to Leaving Care.* RHP, Dorset

Ward, H, Skuse, T (2001) Performance targets and stability of placements for children looked after away from home. *Children and Society* 15(5): 333–346.

Ward, J, Henderson, Z, Pearson, G (2003) *One problem among many: drug use among care leavers in transition to independent living*, Home Office Research Study 260. Home Office, London

West, S (1995) *You're on your own: young people's research on leaving care.* Save the Children, London.

Whitaker, D, Archer, L, Hicks, L (1998) *Working in children's homes, challenges and complexities.* Wiley, Chichester

Who Cares? Trust (1993) *Not just a name: the views of young people in foster and residential care.* National Consumer Council, London.

Wolmar, C (1980) 'Out of care'. *Roof,* March/April. Shelter, London.

Index

university *see* further and higher education
user studies 5–6

victimisation
  of care leavers 52
  see also racism
'victims' group, of care leavers 86–7, 117
voluntary organisations, leaving care services 56,
  57, 60

welfare benefits 17, 68
What happens to foster children? 80–83

Whatever next? 42

young parents 21, 35–8, 74, 81, 84
young people *see* asylum-seeking young people;
  care leavers; disabled young people; looked
  after children; minority ethnic young people
Young People in Transition research (Joseph
  Rowntree Foundation) 109
youth employment *see* employment
youth justice *see* offending
youth training *see* training placements
youth unemployment *see* unemployment